The Cinema of Mia Hansen-Løve

The Cinema of Mia Hansen-Løve

Candour and Vulnerability

Kate Ince

EDINBURGH
University Press

Edinburgh University Press is one of the leading university presses in the UK. We publish academic books and journals in our selected subject areas across the humanities and social sciences, combining cutting-edge scholarship with high editorial and production values to produce academic works of lasting importance. For more information visit our website: edinburghuniversitypress.com

We are committed to making research available to a wide audience and are pleased to be publishing Platinum Open Access editions of the ebooks in this series.

Edinburgh University Press Ltd
The Tun – Holyrood Road
12 (2f) Jackson's Entry
Edinburgh EH8 8PJ

Typeset in 12/14 Arno and Myriad by
IDSUK (DataConnection) Ltd, and
printed and bound by CPI Group (UK) Ltd,
Croydon, CR0 4YY

A CIP record for this book is available from the British Library

ISBN 978 1 4744 6247 1 (hardback)
ISBN 978 1 4744 4767 6 (paperback)
ISBN 978 1 4744 4766 9 (webready PDF)
ISBN 978 1 4744 4768 3 (epub)

Contents

Figures

Acknowledgements

I would like first to thank those UK film academics whose stimulating papers and articles on Mia Hansen-Løve's films, delivered and published while I was still an interested spectator wondering which filmmaker to write about next, inspired me to undertake this book project. Catherine Wheatley, in particular, kindly sent me the pre-print version of her article on Hansen-Løve's post-secular 'search for God'.

Two terms' study leave granted by the University of Birmingham's College of Arts and Law in 2018–19 allowed me to draft the majority of the book's chapters, read the French press reviews of Hansen-Løve's films in the Cinémathèque Française's Bibliothèque du Film, and (on a separate visit to Paris) see *Maya* when it was released in December 2018. I first gave a conference paper on Hansen-Løve at the invigorating Women's Film and Television History Network's May 2018 conference in Southampton, and would like to thank Angelos Koutsourakis for inviting me to speak about *Father of My Children* at the University of Leeds in October 2018, and Dario Llinares and his fellow organisers of the 2019 Film-Philosophy conference at the University of Brighton for accommodating a further paper drawn from draft material. A differently titled version of Chapter 2 has been published in issue 24: 2 of *Film-Philosophy* in July 2020, and I thank the anonymous readers of this article for the various improvements their recommendations allowed me to make.

Finally, I would like to thank Saskia Brown and Martin O'Shaughnessy for valuable exchanges about various of Hansen-Løve's films, Lucy Bolton and Richard Rushton for being stalwart series editors of 'Visionaries', and Gillian Leslie and Richard Strachan at Edinburgh University Press for their support, encouragement and professionalism.

Introduction: Mia Hansen-Løve, transnational auteur

With the release of *Maya* at the 2018 Toronto International Film Festival, Mia Hansen-Løve brought to six the number of feature films she had directed in twelve years, a remarkable achievement for a woman in any film industry. It is one equalled by very few other French women directors,[1] and the mark of a productivity that is even more impressive when we consider that Hansen-Løve is only just forty (she was born in 1981) and that her seventh film is being released as she reaches that birthday. Equally noteworthy is the consistent critical success her films have met with, both domestically and internationally, and the awards they have won, which range from the Prix Louis Delluc for Best First Film in 2007 (shared with Céline Sciamma for *Waterlilies/Naissance des pieuvres*), via the Special Jury prize in the Cannes film festival's Un Certain regard competition in 2009, to the Berlin Silver Bear for Best Director in 2016.

Over just a dozen years, Hansen-Løve has gained a reputation as the director of emotionally rich and insightful dramas that often draw on her life experience but could not be called 'autobiographical', dramas that possess a characteristic lucidity and an idiosyncratically patient approach to narrative. Her initial route into filmmaking was very much that of an auteur (in the attenuated twenty-first-century sense I discuss in **Becoming an auteur** below), and the authorial 'signature' of her filmmaking seems ripe for consideration at this point in her career. In accordance with this objective, this introduction will first outline

Hansen-Løve's route into cinema and the time she spent as a critic for *Cahiers du cinéma* between 2003 and 2005. It will then explore the kind of director she is turning out to be, and consider how her authorship relates to her gender. It will also suggest that although Hansen-Løve, who started her cinematic career as an actor, is in many ways a true insider of French cinema, she is best viewed as a transnational director entirely open to the traditions, influences and industries of many major film-producing nations inside and outside Europe.

Hansen-Løve as actor and critic

As mentioned above, Hansen-Løve's first exposure to cinema was in front of rather than behind the camera, when as a result of an opportunity offered by the drama teacher at her high school (*lycée*), she participated in auditions for, and was cast in, Olivier Assayas's film *Late August, Early September/Fin août, début septembre* (1998). Mathieu Amalric, Jeanne Balibar, Virginie Ledoyen and other well-known French actors starred in this drama about a group of young adults clustered around the middle-aged writer Adrien (François Cluzet), who is suffering from an illness that will prove fatal. While the film focuses more on the younger adults' relationships than on Adrien's, Hansen-Løve, looking the particularly *gamine* teenager that she then was, plays the important role of the girlfriend whose existence Adrien does not reveal to his friends over the last months of his life. Although this part does not seem to have been especially important to Hansen-Løve, the shoot most certainly was, as she repeatedly describes it in interviews in almost epiphanic terms, as *traumatisante* (traumatic) but in a good sense,[2] an experience that decided her once and for all on a career in film.[3] The senses of involvement and belonging she found during the filming of *Late August, Early September* became feelings she absolutely had to experience again - something she did not do until she came to direct a film of her own some years later.

Two years after *Late August, Early September* Hansen-Løve had a small role in another of Assayas's films, *Les Destinées/Les destinées sentimentales* (2000), a long and beautifully located drama about a Protestant pastor in turn-of-the-century Charente (Charles Berling) who faces scandal for divorcing his over-severe wife (Isabelle Huppert) but then resigns the ministry, remarries to the young and independently minded Pauline (Emmanuelle Béart) and devotes the rest of his life to running the family porcelain company. Hansen-Løve was serious enough about acting at this point to enrol for training at France's Conservatoire National Supérieur d'Arts Dramatiques (CNSAD), but left after two years, in 2003, seemingly because her interest in directing was gaining the upper hand. During this period Hansen-Løve made 'three or four' short films of which she says 'none . . . has had a very distinguished career, with the possible exception of the first one' (Jones 2010: 56), titled *After Much Thought/Après mûre refléxion* (2004). Hansen-Løve's favourite of her shorts, *Isabelle By Herself* (2004), 'was more experimental: a silent, poetic portrait of a woman she knew, which she shot in a park in black-and-white 16mm' (2010: 56).[4]

In the early 2000s France's leading film journal *Cahiers du cinéma* had been through a difficult period during which, after coming under the direct control of the country's leading daily newspaper *Le Monde*, it had attempted a makeover and expanded coverage that did not find favour with its traditional readership. In 2003 the film critic and academic Jean-Michel Frodon was appointed chief editor (which he would remain until 2009), and at this point Hansen-Løve became one of *Cahiers*' regular critics for a period of two years, authoring no fewer than fifty-seven articles between issues 580 (July 2003) and 606 (September 2005). Attempting to comment on too many of these would serve no useful purpose, since Hansen-Løve presumably had limited freedom to choose which titles she would review, so after picking out a couple of individual reviews of well-known or popular films, I shall identify two categories of film (by region and genre respectively) that recur among the fifty-seven articles, then comment in more detail on some reviews that anticipate the concerns and characteristics of the feature films Hansen-Løve would go on to direct.

Woody Allen's *Match Point* (2005), which was screened out of competition at the Cannes film festival of 2005 then released in five European countries later that year and more widely early in 2006, was described by Hansen-Løve in her review as 'the least "jazz" and the most "opera" of Woody Allen's films',[5] both anticipating and concurring with the critical acclaim the film went on to meet with internationally. She was equally complimentary, however, about the French comedy *Palais Royal!* (2005), directed by Valérie Lemercier and starring Lemercier, Lambert Wilson and Catherine Deneuve. One of numerous French comedies produced each year and not released outside Europe (where it did travel to Spain, Portugal and Greece), *Palais Royal!* was praised by Hansen-Løve for its cinematography (Lemercier's 'pseudo-discreet' technique of drawing attention to the objective importance of her character to the film by making herself 'falsely small' within the frame), for the precision of its dialogue, and for its 'pitiless observation' of character types.[6]

Asia is a region of the world's cinemas covered by a number of Hansen-Løve's *Cahiers* articles. In 'The Mekong seen from the Ticino', a review of a selection of films from Indochina that were screened at the 2005 Locarno film festival, she considers heavily state-controlled Vietnamese historical films directed by Bui Dinh Hac and Dang Nhat Minh, and reports on a number of titles made by His Majesty the King of Cambodia, Norodom Sihanouk, which she describes as 'both worse – if possible – and more appealing than state-controlled Vietnamese cinema'.[7] During the previous year, 2004, a moment at which China was really only beginning to open up its film culture to the rest of the world, she covered the seventh Shanghai film festival for *Cahiers* and reported on Tian Zhang-zhuang's *Delamu* and Zhu Wen's *South of the Clouds* (two independent films that stood out among a lot of predictable fare) as well as a debate about 'the Chinese phenomenon' (the new generation of Chinese directors) involving Jia Zhangke and Wang Xiao-shuai as well as Zhu Wen, alongside three specialist critics from the US, Japan and Korea.[8] In April of 2004 she reviewed Yu Lik-wai's experimental fiction *All Tomorrow's Parties* in an article entitled 'Zone Chine'.[9]

It is hardly surprising that contemporary experimental and avant-garde cinema is one of the modes of film Hansen-Løve wrote about for *Cahiers*. In November 2003, the veteran Lithuanian-American filmmaker Jonas Mekas was invited to the Centre d'art contemporain de Basse-Normandie at Hérouville Saint-Clair in the outskirts of Caen, in central northern France, for a retrospective of his films included in an event dedicated to Lithuanian art and film. Mekas presented an installation titled 'Dedicated to Fernand Léger . . .' which according to Hansen-Løve was uncharacteristically but pleasingly cacophonous, full of the noise of children (Mekas's own) shouting, phones ringing, fire engine sirens, trumpets, applause and so on.[10] In the February 2004 edition of *Cahiers*, the full interview with Mekas she had carried out in Hérouville Saint-Clair was published, in which Mekas talked about his entire career and his tastes in popular film (Clint Eastwood, westerns, and action films), as well as the films of Andy Warhol and John Cassavetes.[11] A few months later Hansen-Løve wrote about the annual Festival Nemo of experimental film at Paris's Forum des Images, an event featuring video art, 2D/3D animation, motion graphic design, video games, internet art and interactive cinema. Her review notes that the works presented were heavily oriented towards developing technologies, raising questions such as 'Does technological performance have an absolute aesthetic value?' and implying that this festival is progressively reinterpreting 'experimental' in a technological sense.[12] 'Although it would be ridiculous to oppose art to technology', Hansen-Løve remarks, 'it would be just as naïve to marvel at films only remarkable for the perfection of their technique'.[13]

A filmmaker who might be termed 'experimental' in a more traditional sense and about whom Hansen-Løve wrote twice for *Cahiers* is Jean-Pierre Gorin, Jean-Luc Godard's collaborator in the Dziga Vertov group from 1968 to 1972. Gorin, who emigrated to California in the mid-1970s, returned to directing with 'the marvellous *Poto and Cabengo*'[14] in 1978, one of three of his films featured in the 2004 Viennale (Vienna film festival). Hansen-Løve's article about the festival (she also reviewed *Poto and Cabengo* separately in a later issue[15]) marvels at the smoothness of Gorin's transition from French to American film culture revealed in his US-based trilogy, each film in which 'is a way of penetrating further into American space – geographical, linguistic, mental'.[16] Gorin also reproduced the structure of his collaboration with Godard in the US by developing a partnership with Manny Farber, about which little is known in France, an omission that the remainder of Hansen-Løve's article starts to remedy.

It is in two *Cahiers* articles about American directors Michael Mann and Larry Clark that concerns germane to Hansen-Løve's own films can be found – her article on Mann, punningly titled 'Mann's women' [*Femmes de Mann*] considers male-female couples in *Ali* (2001), *Collateral* (2004) and *Heat* (1995), while her review of Clark's *Ken Park* (2002) appears in a dossier of articles that starts with a roundtable discussion of *Ken Park*, Clint Eastwood's *Mystic River* and Gus Van Sant's *Elephant*, all films that concerned the lives of American teenagers and were released in France in October 2004. Affirming that Larry Clark's sole artistic project is 'to invent a myth of adolescence'[17], the core of Hansen-Løve's analysis of *Ken Park* runs as follows:

> Of all Larry Clark's films, *Ken Park* is the most Oedipal, in its phobias of the father, of a morality made of paternal virility, and of the father's timeworn authority and murky desires. By contrast, teenagers' sexual ideal is a fatherless ideal. But because he has created the myth of their generation – the *kids* – Larry Clark means to take on the role of father himself, a putative father for these self-proclaimed orphans. To take on this role, he offers them a re-appropriation of their image [the character Ken Park], albeit one of a suicide case.[18]

She concludes by describing Clark as 'the most serious and perhaps the only emblem of today's American counterculture, in the sense that he opposes a sub-culture to a society and its mass culture that is both the negative and the product of that society and culture'.[19] Clark's on-screen world cannot be recuperated by 'the adult world' and is stuck in something like a Freudian repetition compulsion: all Ken Park's suicide achieves is a shutting-down of 'the ineluctable logic of the reproduction of the same'.[20] Of Michael Mann, Hansen-Løve's view is that Mann's reputation as a filmer of confrontations between men does not mean that the women in his films are insignificant: their roles are certainly secondary to the men, but not purely functional, since in her estimation Mann shares Quentin Tarantino's 'acute vision'[21] [*regard aigu*] of women. Women may be entirely excluded from the action of *Heat*, but Mann achieves an impressive tragic vision of male-female relationships across at least five couples, while in *Ali*, Nona Gaye, Jada Pinkett Smith and Michael Michele play female characters who offer 'remarkable antidotes to Hollywood's Halle Berry types'[22] through their mature relationships with Ali (Will Smith). In *Collateral* a woman, Annie (Jada Pinkett Smith) is important to the plot of a Mann film for the first time, and although this might be put down to Mann not having written the film himself, Hansen-Løve still finds his directorial vision in the lengthy early scene that introduces Annie as a character. In Mann's films, 'women stand out because of their discretion and their strength of character'[23], and he does not film young ingénues or make his female characters' intelligence serve only the plot.

The interest in adolescent lives and mature male-female relationships that would emerge in Hansen-Løve's own films is thus already apparent in the articles on independent American directors she wrote for *Cahiers*, and other concerns of her filmmaking can be detected in her reviews of French filmmakers such as Gérard Blain (the father of Paul Blain, who would play Victor in *All Is Forgiven/Tout est pardonné*) and Jacques Doillon. Gérard Blain made just nine films between 1971 and his death in 2000, and it is the third, *A Child in the Crowd/Un enfant dans la foule* (1976) that Hansen-Løve takes as a focus for her discussion of how Blain was influenced by Robert Bresson (a director she herself admires) and of 'great films about childhood', of which she sees *A Child in the Crowd* as the last in a series that began with Truffaut's *The 400 Blows/Les quatre cents coups* (1959). The vision of childhood conveyed in *A Child in the Crowd* is by far the bleakest of the series, with a 'stone-hearted'[24] mother who incomprehensibly but deeply hates her son Paul, and a father who is indifferent to him and leaves the family. Its fascination with difficult relationships between fathers and sons means that Blain's cinema evinces what Roland Barthes called 'the inverse Oedipus complex'.[25] In an article on Doillon's *The Prodigal Daughter/La fille prodigue* (1980), shown at a 2005 retrospective of films starring Jane Birkin, Hansen-Løve's interest in dysfunctional parent-child relationships is even clearer, although this time it is the relationship between a daughter, Anne (Jane Birkin), and her father (Michel Piccoli), and a positive rather than a negative Oedipus complex – in the film, Anne leaves her husband and returns to the parental home, where she gives free rein to an incestuous desire for her father. What is interesting about Hansen-Løve's appraisal of *The Prodigal Daughter* is that despite her awareness of the 'psychoanalytic charge'[26] of the film (in which Anne exhausts her father with her possessive jealousy and he eventually collapses onto his back on the floor and 'offers himself as if in sacrifice to his daughter'[27]), she seems to find Piccoli's performance and physique its most memorable aspects, remarking on 'the carnal beauty of Piccoli's massive body' and on his 'superb fragility' and 'the eroticism of his goodness'.[28] In Hansen-Løve's view, the film both bears out Freudian theory and frees itself of it through the personal deliverance that Anne experiences by committing incest with her father: it is Anne's words when this act takes place, 'I have found the man I come from' [*J'ai retrouvé l'homme dont je viens*] that Hansen-Løve uses as the title of her article.

When Hansen-Løve's début feature film *All Is Forgiven/Tout est pardonné*, which she reports writing in the winter of 2003,[29] was released in 2007 and selected for competition at Cannes, *Cahiers du cinéma* invited her to present the film in its pages, introducing her as one of its 'former critics' – although she has in fact continued to publish in it occasionally, and to be interviewed about her films. Hansen-Løve's assessment of this intensive period spent writing criticism is that there was a 'question of principle' at stake: if one wants to practise an art (and she knew she wanted to direct films), it is essential not to be preoccupied only by one's own work and to study other practitioners' work closely.[30] Even although she found the conception of cinema that prevailed at *Cahiers* too ideological for her liking, the work of criticism was helpful 'in achieving a certain clarity'. 'Writing helps you focus and makes you get down to the essentials', she comments.[31]

Becoming an auteur

Hansen-Løve's period of full-time employment at *Cahiers du cinéma* may have been relatively short, but it is impossible not to observe how similar it makes her route into feature filmmaking to the early careers of François Truffaut, Jean-Luc Godard, and the other young men of France's Nouvelle Vague. What most obviously differentiates her from them, of course, is her gender, but assessing how important this difference is and how it may be colouring her success as a filmmaker is a task beset by several difficulties. First, there is the relatively high proportion of feature films directed by women in France as compared to other European and non-European countries, which commentators are often at a loss to explain, even if it seems to indicate that a positive context exists for women seeking to direct and produce in Francophone territory (that is, in France's overseas departments and collectivities as well as its mainland, though there is little film-making activity in any of the former). Second, there is the non-validity across that territory of the category of 'female authorship', which has become an increasing focus of Anglophone (feminist) film commentary since the late 1980s. Third, there is Hansen-Løve's own ambivalence towards the significance of her gender as a factor in her filmmaking: this is an issue on which she has sometimes commented, but in a distinctly non-committal fashion. In order to shed some light on Hansen-Løve's status as a contemporary French woman auteur, I shall discuss each of these areas in turn.

Since the 'watershed' decade of the 1970s for women's filmmaking worldwide, when women began to direct in significant numbers for the first time, their share of annual production in France has increased steadily from less than 10% in the 1980s to 13.7% in the 1990s (Tarr with Rollet 2001: 3) and 18.3% in the 2000s (Tarr 2012: 190–1). Against an increased overall level of production, the absolute number of films directed by women more than doubled from an average seventeen films per year in the 1990s to an average of thirty-six in the 2000s (Tarr 2012: 190–1), reaching more than forty per annum in the last four years of the decade. Although 18.3% in the 2000s and a probable proportion of between 20% and 25% in the 2010s[32] is nowhere near the parity aimed at by campaigns such as '50:50 by 2020',[33] it is well above the figures achieved in Hollywood and most other national cinemas. Hansen-Løve, who released two feature films in the 2000s and four in the 2010s, is a leading contributor to the steadily increasing share of film production that women are gaining in her native country. Of course, whether the gender of their director is detectably marked in her films, either in their narratives or aesthetically, is a separate question from the gender-political context in which she works, and is a question I shall sometimes touch on in the chapters of this book and shall return to in its conclusion.

If female authorship of the kind now frequently discussed in Anglophone film writing poses a problem in the French context, this is for a political reason that is more internationally visible where France's ethnic/racial minorities are concerned, in the wearing of signs of religious adherence like the Muslim veil and the Jewish kippah, which is still outlawed in public arenas such as schools and colleges despite being increasingly contested in recent decades. 'Advertising' religious adherence in this way goes against the notion of citizenship implied in French secular Republicanism, according to which each individual citizen is equal in their neutrality, a kind of 'absolute equality', and the state does not recognise or interact with communities or groups united by racial, ethnic, religious or linguistic identity. Identity politics of the kind familiar from the US and UK is referred to as *communautarisme*, and is viewed as a threat to the Republican tradition presently actualised (since 1958) in the Fifth Republic. Women, of course, are not a minority statistically, but because feminism can be viewed as a form of identity politics, it is classified as a type of *communautarisme* at odds with the state's citizenship policies. Resistance to identity politics in France, exacerbated in recent years in debates about gay marriage, which was legalised in 2013, undermines the confidence with which women and minorities can 'advertise' their qualified kind of identity: whatever their individual view about the importance of their femaleness, blackness or religious practice to their occupation (since it is in the public sphere that awareness of *communautarisme* is strongest), drawing attention to it is a less straightforward matter than in many other countries.

The Francophone film world is obviously not immune to the political sensitivities affecting French society as a whole, and it is therefore to be expected that film authorship will be affected by the resistance to identity politics outlined above. In France as elsewhere, the category of the auteur, which fell out of favour in the 1970s and 1980s before making a contested recovery in the globalised 1990s, has survived into twenty-first-century film criticism, but in France it has not 'diversified' along the same lines as in the Anglophone world. Awareness of the femaleness, non-normative sexuality or non-whiteness of the director of a film certainly exists in France, but is not mediatised as intensively or accepted as politically significant as easily as in many other places. Whereas Anglophone film writers are now accustomed to employing 'female', 'gay' and 'black' to qualify the authorship of whatever film(s) they are discussing (though they may not agree it is important to do so), this does not occur with any regularity or consistency in French film criticism. How, then, does this climate influence Hansen-Løve's work as a French woman director?

As suggested above, the French Republican model undoubtedly influences women's cultural production in France: it does not necessarily impede or suppress women's creativity or self-expression, of course, but through being ingrained in the very way women think about their social identity, it affects their willingness to identify as 'feminist' or to qualify their work as gendered, in whatever way. An article entitled 'We Women' [*Nous, les femmes*] that Hansen-Love wrote for *Cahiers du cinéma* 681, an issue largely given over to a dossier on women directors worldwide, reveals both these tensions and her response to them (Hansen-Løve 2012: 28–9). In the short final paragraph of the article she poses two questions that could be described as summarising the dilemma of women directors working in France, stuck between female specificity and Republican universalism: 'What is a female [*féminin*] vision of the world? What is a vision of the world?' (2012: 29). By stating a preference for the second question, because, she says, it seems to allow her 'to open a window and to breathe' (2012: 29), Hansen-Løve repeats a move made by countless French women directors since the 1970s – a preference for a non-gender-specific directing identity. However, she reaches this conclusion after demonstrating a thoroughgoing awareness of her situation, commenting, for example, that she is 'systematically' asked by Anglophone critics about the *difference* (original emphasis) of women's filmmaking and what comprises it (2012: 28). She makes a distinction between the political and artistic dimensions of gender identity faced by filmmakers, answering a decisive 'yes' to the need to discuss women's difficulties in getting to direct and to helping them do so, but 'no' to approaching film texts in the light of a director's femaleness. She is evidently very aware of *communautarisme*, despite only using the term once, when she is describing the tendency of contemporary societies and film audiences to become increasingly divided into 'sociological groups' (*tranches sociologiques*) or 'communities' (*communautés*) based on gender or ethnic identity (2012: 29). This tendency oppresses her, she reports, producing 'a suffocating feeling' (*sensation d'étouffement*) (2012: 29).

It may not be accurate to interpret the views Hansen-Løve explains in 'We Women' as a refusal to identify as a 'woman filmmaker', because the question is not put to her in these terms. 'Female authorship' is a contested critical and theoretical concept she is unlikely to be familiar with, precisely because of her working context. And however much her career path resembles those of Truffaut and other filmmaker-critics originally involved in defining what it means to be an auteur, it also has elements in common with many contemporary women directors – her discovery of the desire to direct through acting, for example. Whereas the mode of authorship championed by the Nouvelle Vague's filmmaker-critics emphasised an expansive originality and creativity, Hansen-Løve insists on the importance of studying other filmmakers' work in order to better hone her personal style, which is evidently one she examines critically. Perhaps most importantly, reluctance to identify as a 'woman filmmaker' does not in any way reduce the sense of solidarity she evidently feels with other women, whatever their occupation: 'It's not that I don't feel in solidarity with the problems women face in the world. More than ever, this cause too is mine' (Hansen-Løve 2012: 29). Does such solidarity add up to a kind of feminism? Whether it does or not, Hansen-Løve's expressed readiness to be an ally of women's struggles draws attention to her strong awareness of her femaleness, which she articulates early in 'We Women' as she addresses the question 'Does a women's cinema exist?' 'Certainly, the fact that I am a woman is connected to everything I feel, write and shoot. It is part of me, and, I'm very aware, affects everything I undertake' (2012: 29). This statement is directly followed by a reported one that comparing two women filmmakers is likely to reveal as much in common as between Mahatma Gandhi and Mahmoud Ahmadinejad, but Hansen-Løve's words are still striking in their force. She may not want to endorse the widely used Anglophone notion of 'women's cinema', employed to politicise the female gender of film directors rather than to refer to any properties shared by films directed by women, but she recognises and accepts that her gender cannot be neutralised, and that this affects her professional as well as her personal identity.

Transnational authorship in contemporary France

The analysis of Hansen-Løve's mode of authorship offered above omits one important dimension of its character during her career to date – the transnational one. Being of partly Danish descent, Hansen-Løve may be more 'European' in her influences and connections than some French filmmakers, but whether this internationalism can be attributed to her family background or not, characters and locations from outside France feature regularly in her films. The first part of *All Is Forgiven* (2007) takes place in Vienna, the home of Austrian Annette (Marie-Christine Friedrich), who remarries another Frenchman after the breakdown of her relationship with Victor (Paul Blain) charted in the film. German (appropriately subtitled) is spoken in several scenes. In *Father of My Children/Le père de mes enfants* (2009), Hansen-Løve's fictional version of the life of film producer Humbert Balsan sees him married to the Italian Sylvia (Chiara Caselli) where in reality his wife was American. A little Italian is spoken in the film, and several important scenes take place in and around ecclesiastical buildings in Ravenna on a family holiday. Although only a few scenes of *Goodbye First Love* (2011) take place outside France, when viewing architectural sites in Denmark and Germany that are important for Camille (Lola Créton)'s training, the teacher of architecture who comes to replace her 'first love' Sullivan, Lorenz, is played by Norwegian actor Magne Håvard-Brekke who also played the role of 'genius' auteur director Stig Larsen in *Father of My Children*, and is understood to be Scandinavian or of Scandinavian descent. *Eden*, the fiction about house and garage music of the 1990s that Hansen-Løve co-wrote with her brother Sven, on whom the character of Paul (Félix de Givry) is based, is probably her most international story to date, because the musicians and DJs featured in the film are as often American as they are French, and going on tour to New York is a key professional achievement for Paul and his DJ-ing partner Stan (Hugo Conzelmann). A lot of English is spoken in the film, and the serious girlfriend Paul has at its start is the American Julia (Greta Gerwig). In comparison with these first four features, *Things to Come/L'Avenir* is particularly French and France-bound, but with *Maya* Hansen-Løve moves beyond Europe and the West for the first time by setting the great majority of the film in Goa, India.

This catalogue of languages and locations outside Hansen-Løve's native France demonstrates an unquestionable trans-nationalism on her part: she may have followed a particularly French career path into film, but she is anything but blinkered in her approach to story-writing and casting, and is as open to diverse countries and cultures as one might expect of a 'millennial' born in 1981. Transnationalism also features in the financing and production of Hansen-Løve's films, although here it is just the European Union's MEDIA programme, the German Federal Film Board (*Filmförderungsanstalt* (FFA)) and two other German companies, the Berlin-Brandenburg Media Board and Razor Film Ltd, that have been significant players. (A large number of France-based production companies including Les Films Pelléas, the CNC, and regions such as Ile-de-France, the Limousin and Rhône-Alpes have been majority funders in Hansen-Løve's various film projects.)

As film scholar Gemma King comments in her recent book *Decentering France*, transnational cinema studies has achieved a great deal in a short period of time where accounting for the complex structures of today's global film industries is concerned. It may only have taken off in the twenty-first century, but by offering 'a means through which to discuss films marked by international aspects, without ignoring the concept of the national' (King 2017: 12), transnational film studies can elucidate bodies of work such as that of Hansen-Løve as well as the constantly shifting character of the 'French' film industry. The particular focus of *Decentering France* is multilingual cinema, which King defines not simply as films employing more than one language occasionally or casually,[34] a common practice throughout the twentieth century as well as in the twenty-first, but films in which multiple language use equates to the exercise of power, through practices such as code-switching – films that 'uncover the many possible fields of social power at play in multilingual scenes' (2017: 4). Despite the regular occurrence of languages other than French (German, Italian, English) in Hansen-Løve's cinema to date, her films do not in my view belong in the same category as the multilingual French films discussed in *Decentering France*, which 'resist monopolistic centrings of authority and situate multiple language use within correspondingly polycentric French and global spaces' (2017: 4). Hansen-Løve's films can be described as multilingual, since they – like their director – are culturally polyglot, but social power relations are not at stake in their use of languages other than French, even in *Maya* where Indian languages are spoken alongside the British English in which all educated Indians are fluent. It is noteworthy that the languages spoken in addition to French in Hansen-Løve's films are mainly European languages and American and British English, rather than the tongues of France's postcolonial subjects (Arabic, Berber) or of migrants from other regions of the globe.

If the non-French languages and nationalities that feature in Hansen-Løve's films do not connote power relations, this may disqualify her from any status as a political director (which, as became evident in the previous section, she does not aspire to anyway). It does, however, place her in an ever-growing category of globally literate French directors identified by Alice Burgin, Andrew McGregor and Colin Nettelbeck as 'a transnational auteur cinema emerging from France that extends the traditional concept of cultural diversity beyond French/European borders, incorporating transcultural narratives and promoting various forms of *cinémas du monde*' (Burgin, McGregor and Nettelbeck 2014: 397, quoted in King 2017: 9). A large part of the value of transnational film studies has been to dismantle rather than take an axe to the older paradigm of 'monolithic' national cinemas, 'acknowledging instead the diverse cultural exchanges which occur in film narratives and cinematic production practices' (King 2017: 9). Although the paradigm of national cinemas now appears outdated, it has not been entirely displaced and is certainly not worthless: it is still meaningful to speak of 'French cinema' – and describe a filmmaker such as Hansen-Løve as 'a French director' – in the early 2020s. As King writes to conclude the 'French cinema' section of her introduction to *Decentering France*: 'To speak of a French cinema is not to box French films into a narrow, monocultural definition, but to acknowledge the plurality of voices, identities and modes of production that characterise the cinema of twenty-first century France' (2017: 15).

The book

The discussions of Hansen-Løve's films that follow are structured into six chapters, on the family (Chapter 1, *Fracture familiale*); on vulnerability or vulnerabilisation (Chapter 2, Vulnerable people); on the marked work ethic demonstrated by all the films' leading protagonists which, following Catherine Wheatley (Wheatley 2019) I see as post-secular (Chapter 3, Adversity and resilience: the post-secular ethic of vocation); on the importance of a certain 'spirituality' and experiences of transcendence to the films (Chapter 4, Candid camera, or an aesthetic of transcendence); on music (Chapter 5, Lost in music); and finally, on time (Chapter 6, The rivers of time). The criticism of other Anglophone commentators on Hansen-Løve's cinema such as Wheatley, Emma Wilson and Fiona Handyside has been vital to the approach I have developed to Hansen-Løve's work, which is to see her as an ethical filmmaker – or more precisely, as a filmmaker possessed of an ethical vision that emerges through the themes (many of them 'moral' qualities such as vulnerability, resilience and candour) around which the book is organised. I introduce ethics towards the end of Chapter 1, focus on it in Chapters 2 and 3, then concentrate on the films' aesthetics in Chapters 4 and 5, before returning to ethics in relation to time and temporality in Chapter 6. A conclusion then draws together the explorations undertaken in the six chapters.

Notes

All translations, unless otherwise stated, are the author's own.

1 According to a report produced by the CNC in 2017, only three women (Hansen-Løve, Julie Delpy and Anne Fontaine) had directed more than four films in the decade between 2006 and 2015, although thirty-five had directed at least three, with some of these only releasing their first film in 2009. See 'La place des femmes dans l'industrie cinématographique et audiovisuelle' on the CNC website at <https://www.cnc.fr/cinema/etudes-et-rapports/etudes-prospectives/la-place-des-femmes-dans-lindustrie-cinematographique-et-audiovisuelle_300828>.

2 *Hors Champs* of 20 May 2010, broadcast on France Culture.

3 Hansen-Løve's love of cinema began with the encounter with Assayas that this shoot offered her, she initially explains to Laure Adler in the same radio interview.

4 This film is on YouTube at <https://www.youtube.com/watch?v=5wz93DlP2Sc> (last accessed 18 August 2019), where it seems to have been titled *A Pure Mind/ Un pur esprit* by YouTube despite actually being called *Isabelle par elle-même*. It is not silent, as sounds and noise are heard throughout, but has no dialogue or speech; the few words spoken by Isabelle are inaudible.

5 'Echec et smash', *Cahiers du cinéma* 605 (July 2005), 28–9. The title of the review, which translates literally as 'Defeat and smash', puns on the French for 'checkmate', 'échec et mat'.

6 'Offensive sur les bords', *Cahiers du cinéma* 606 (August 2005), 29–30.

7 'Le Mékong vu du Tessin', *Cahiers du cinéma* 593 (September 2004), p. 52.

8 'Shanghai s'entrouvre aux cinéastes indépendants', *Cahiers du cinéma* 592 (July-August 2004), p. 64.

9 'Zone Chine', *Cahiers du cinéma* 589 (April 2004), 23–6.

10 'Jonas Mekas et le son retrouvé', *Cahiers du cinéma* 586 (January 2004), p. 71.

11 'Nous avons besoin d'action', Interview with Jonas Mekas, *Cahiers du cinéma* 587 (February 2004), 74–7.

12 'Exploration aux frontières', *Cahiers du cinéma* 589 (April 2004), 48–9.

13 Ibid. p. 48.

14 Mia Hansen-Løve, 'Des jumelles et des jumeaux', *Cahiers du cinéma* 596 (December 2004), 51–2.

15 Mia Hansen-Løve, 'Cabengo', *Cahiers du cinéma* 598 (February 2005), 76–7.

16 'Des jumelles et des jumeaux', p. 51.

17 Mia Hansen-Løve, 'Portraits crachés' (review of *Ken Park*), *Cahiers du cinéma* 583 (October 2003), 23–4.

18 'Portraits crachés', p. 23.

19 Ibid. p. 24.

20 Ibid. p. 24.

21 Mia Hansen-Løve, 'Femmes de Mann', *Cahiers du cinéma* 597 (January 2005), 80–1 (p. 80).

22 Ibid. p. 80.

23 Ibid. p. 80.

24 Mia Hansen-Løve, 'Les passants et les passeurs', *Cahiers du cinéma* 604 (September 2005), 89–90 (p. 90).

25 Ibid. p. 90.

26 Mia Hansen-Løve, 'J'ai retrouvé l'homme dont je viens', *Cahiers du cinéma* 607 (December 2005), p. 34

27 Ibid. p. 34.

28 Ibid. p. 34.

29 *Cahiers du cinéma* 623 (May 2007), p. 22.

30 Axel Zeppenfeld, 'Entretien avec Mia Hansen-Løve', *Cahiers du cinéma* 627 (October 2007), p. 21.

31 Richard Porton, 'A Death in the Family: an Interview with Mia Hansen-Løve', *Cineaste* 35: 3 (Summer 2010), 10–14 (p. 14).

32 According to Charlotte Pudlowski in an article about the complete absence of films directed by women from the main competition at Cannes in 2012, 52 such films – a massive 25 per cent of the total – were released in 2011 (Pudlowski 2012).

33 See <https://en.wikipedia.org/wiki/5050x2020> and #5050x2020 on social media.

34 King attributes the pinpointing of 'minor or superficial instances of multilingualism in cinema' to Chris Wahl, who calls it 'postcarding' in 'Discovering a Genre: the Polyglot Film', *Cinemascope* 1: 1 (2005), 1–8 (King 2017: 6).

1

Fracture familiale

Broken and 'recomposed' families are found in all Hansen-Løve's films, and although the absence of a father from the families of *Goodbye First Love* and *Eden* (where mothers figure significantly) is not obviously paining their young protagonists Camille and Paul, the effects of family crisis are the main subject of *All Is Forgiven*, *Father of My Children* and *Things to Come*, and an important secondary subject of *Maya*. In *All Is Forgiven*, the marriage of Annette and Victor breaks down, and Annette takes Pamela (Victoire Rousseau) to South America for a sufficiently long period that they cannot be traced upon their subsequent return to Paris, where Victor remains, dealing with his drug addiction. Following the suicide of charismatic film producer Grégoire Canvel (Louis-Do de Lencquesaing), the entire second half of *Father of My Children* follows the contrasting adjustments to his death made by his wife Sylvia and eldest daughter Clémence (Alice de Lencquesaing), who only now discovers that she has a half-brother from Grégoire's first marriage. *Things to Come*'s Nathalie (Isabelle Huppert) has to deal with her husband Heinz (André Marcon)'s infidelity and departure and her unstable mother's final decline and death at the same time, and in *Maya*, Gabriel (Roman Kolinka)'s recovery from four months' captivity as a hostage in Syria takes place against the backdrop of a recognition that his family is irrecoverably divided between France and India.

The expression *fracture sociale* was coined by French President Jacques Chirac in 1995 to describe the faultlines weakening the fabric of French society, and was subsequently adopted into French discourse as shorthand for the nation's most troubling divisions. (Since the failure to integrate the second- and third-generation families of (post)colonial immigrants from the Maghreb and Sub-Saharan Africa was and remains primary among these, it is not surprising that the term *fracture coloniale* was also coined subsequently, in 2006.[1]) The expression *fracture familiale* does not seem to have been used about French society except in an ad hoc fashion in journalism, in reference to disputes and rifts in particular families, but describes succinctly the vision of the contemporary family found in Hansen-Løve's cinema, in which a complete nuclear family composed of a father, a mother and one or more children only occurs temporarily: for the majority of each film, one parent (usually the father) is missing due to death, separation or divorce. Remarriage of a parent resulting in what the French term a *famille recomposée* is seen in *All Is Forgiven*, where after leaving Victor, Annette has married André (Pascal Bongard), meaning that Pamela gains a stepbrother and a half-brother, and in *Maya*, where Gabriel's mother Johanna (Johanna Ter Steege), who remained in India after separating from his father when Gabriel was seven, now has children with her second husband. In *All Is Forgiven*, *Father of My Children* and *Things to Come*, what the film charts is this damaging change to the family's structure and how its members adjust to it.

Changes to family structure of this kind are obviously not confined to France, but are typical of late twentieth- and twenty-first-century Western societies, where the number of adults living alone has been rising steadily for decades, cohabitation has become as common as actual marriage and divorce rates are as high as 50%.[2] In *Liquid Modernity* (2000), sociologist Zygmunt Bauman examines how Western modernity has moved into a 'light' and 'liquid' stage in which, under the influence of capitalist individualism, human bonds themselves have become fragile, and families and communities are less robust and more fragmented than in the period before the Second World War. Bauman is also the author of *Liquid Love: on the Frailty of Human Bonds* (2003), where he develops the notion of 'liquid' employed in *Liquid Modernity*, applying it specifically to the neighbourly and intimate relationships found in communities and in the family ('togetherness'). As set out above, the *fracture familiale* characterising Hansen-Løve's films shows her to be unusually drawn to charting the emotional consequences of family division and dysfunction on 'children' who are sometimes already adults, in a way that Bauman's idea of 'liquid love' can elucidate. By exploring the tensions and disunity of Hansen-Løve's families alongside Bauman's postmodern sociology, this chapter will explain how *fracture familiale* is a vital part of her twenty-first-century world-view.

Liquid love and the twenty-first-century family

The 'liquidity' of human relationships examined by Bauman in *Liquid Love* refers above all to their temporariness, fragility and substitutability. In tandem with the sexual liberation of the 1960s and the second wave feminism and gay liberation movements of the 1970s and 1980s, marriage laws started to become increasingly liberal across the West, with the first 'no fault' divorces introduced in the US in the 1970s. Sexual freedom for women, gay men and lesbians as well as men lessened both the permanency and seriousness associated with heterosexual marriage, and the institution began to loosen its grip on Western societies, with couples marrying later and separating and divorcing more frequently. (The recent passing of laws in numerous Western countries allowing gay men and lesbians to marry has of course constituted one of the most significant changes to the institution of the family for hundreds of years, but since neither homosexuality nor gay partnerships or marriage figure in any of Hansen-Løve's films, I shall not treat this aspect of the contemporary family in this chapter.) The rise of neoliberal economics from the 1980s onwards reinforced the trends away from large families and extended families living in the same household and towards small nuclear families, single-parent households and single-person households, which at the time of writing number approximately one-third of the total number of households in the EU.

Bauman introduces *Liquid Love* by stating that what the book 'tries to unravel, record and grasp' is '[t]he uncanny frailty of human bonds, the feeling of insecurity that frailty inspires, and the conflicting desires that feeling prompts to tighten the bonds yet keep them loose' (Bauman 2003: viii). In the liquid modern world, we yearn both for the security of togetherness and for the freedoms we have become accustomed to in the (comparatively) affluent West, with its liberal labour laws, developed health and welfare systems and well-remunerated career paths. The result is an ambivalence about long-term, committed relationships such as marriage: '[i]n our world of rampant "individualization" relationships are mixed blessings. They vacillate between sweet dream and a nightmare, and there is no telling when one turns into the other' (2003: viii). This ambivalence is what seems to underlie the largely European societies in which Hansen-Løve's films are set, where one spouse leaves a marriage without their reasons for so doing being dwelt upon, as Camille's father (Serge Renko) does in *Goodbye First Love*. (He has met another woman he prefers to share his life with, and no further justification is necessary.) In *Things to Come*, Nathalie Chazeaux suffers the now stereotypical middle-aged woman's life-change of being left for a younger woman, although she only finds this out when she happens to spot her husband Heinz (André Marcon) with his new partner in the street (Heinz has volunteered no real information about her, and Nathalie does not ask). Nathalie's response to Heinz when he initially breaks the news to her that he is leaving is a wistful '[a]nd there was I thinking that you'd love me for ever!', her irony implying that she was foolish actually to believe in the marriage vows she and Heinz exchanged twenty-five years previously.

Bauman does not devote an entire chapter to the family in *Liquid Love*, but having announced in its Foreword that '[t]he principal hero of this book is human *relationship*' (Bauman 2003: viii), most of its chapters' subjects – love, sociality, the notion of 'loving one's neighbour' and togetherness – impinge directly on the family as a cornerstone of social organisation across cultures worldwide. A key notion to describe what has lost influence in late twentieth-century and twenty-first-century Western societies is *communitas*, treated in the chapter 'In and Out of the Toolbox of Sociality'. Theorised particularly by British anthropologist Victor Turner and his wife Edith, *communitas*, which the Turners qualified in various ways depending on which anthropological phenomena they were describing, is the kind of unstructured state – most often a rite of passage, ritual or ceremony – that allows the whole of a community to share a common experience. *Communitas* is usually associated with the experience of joy,[3] and is inseparable from the human relationships that are sealed or transformed when it is experienced. The increasingly 'developed', technological and bureaucratic societies of the West rely far less on rituals, rites of passage and the forging of human bonds than they did prior to the 1950s, and once changes in human relationships such as coming of age and marriage are no longer accorded symbolic importance by the communities in which they take place, dissolving or reversing the bonds so celebrated is no longer of great consequence. Bauman remarks that the survival and well-being of *communitas* 'depend on human imagination, inventiveness and courage in *breaking* the routine and trying the *untried* ways', and continues:

> They depend, in other words, on the human ability to live with risk and accept responsibility for the consequences. It is these abilities that are the supports for the 'moral economy' – mutual care and help, living *for* the other, weaving the tissue of human commitments, fastening and servicing interhuman bonds. (Bauman 2003: 74)

It is 'the invasion and colonization of *communitas*, the site of the moral economy, by consumer market forces' that 'constitutes the most awesome of dangers threatening the present form of human togetherness' (Bauman 2003: 74). Family togetherness is a primary form of *communitas*, and the fragile and eroded condition in which it is seen to be in Hansen-Løve's film dramas testifies to

Figure 1.1 Victor and Pamela in the Parc des Buttes-Chaumont, Paris, *All Is Forgiven*

the weakening of kinship bonds characteristic of contemporary European societies (Figure 1.1).

Fracture familiale and film form in *All Is Forgiven* and *Father of My Children*

It was widely observed by critics and audiences that Hansen-Løve's first two films share a narrative structure, whose first half follows a nuclear family through the period leading up to a radical shift in that family's structure and fortunes. In *All Is Forgiven* the family breaks up altogether, while in *Father of My Children* Grégoire's suicide leaves his widow Sylvia with the unanticipated work of seeing whether his production company Moon Films can be saved from bankruptcy, and his three daughters with much adjusting to do to their new circumstances. The second half of *Father of My Children* follows Sylvia, Clémence, Valentine and

Billie through the months following Grégoire's death, whereas in *All Is Forgiven*, an ellipsis of eleven years effects a change of protagonist, with the parents giving way to their daughter Pamela, now on the brink of adulthood. In both films, the abrupt change in family structure occurs exactly halfway through the action (at 52 minutes of *All Is Forgiven's* 105 minutes, and 55 minutes into the 110 minutes of *Father of My Children*).

The first half of *All Is Forgiven* is itself divided into two chapters named after their location, 'Vienna, 1995', and 'Return to Paris'. There is a striking contrast between the family's two apartments in the two cities: whereas the Viennese apartment is spacious and light, the one in Paris is much more cramped, with a bathroom and sleeping area that open off the main room, which is a kitchen and living area combined. The initial split between Victor and Annette occurs after an argument in which Victor strikes Annette, who has been out for supper with a male friend in order to get away from Victor's dissolute lifestyle (he drinks at home and in cafés and bars, as well as taking drugs prescribed to him by a doctor). Victor declines the invitation to eat with Annette and the friend, but sits alone in the dark while she is out, then, when she returns at a late hour, remonstrates with her for taking Pamela to eat with 'assholes' (*connards*), strikes her several times across the face, and shouts at her that she has humiliated him. The next morning, husband, wife and daughter eat a subdued breakfast at which Annette cannot look at Victor, but announces she is taking Pamela to Vienna for Christmas, alone. Victor spends Christmas at his friend Zoltan's (Wieland Amand), where he starts an affair with a woman called Gisèle (Olivia Ross), a fellow addict regularly injecting heroin, to which she introduces Victor. He and Annette are briefly reconciled when she returns from Vienna, but do not continue living together, Victor remaining at Zoltan's with Gisèle until she overdoses one night, which precipitates a kind of breakdown in Victor, who is hospitalised. When Annette visits him and they walk together in the hospital grounds he asks if she can forgive him, to which – after a long pause during which she starts to cry – Annette replies 'I don't think so'. She repeats these words, and tells Victor she is taking Pamela to Caracas, Venezuela, where she has been offered a job. The *coup de grâce* follows when she says 'Victor, I don't ever want to see you again', words which conclusively end their marriage, without future access to Pamela on Victor's part ever being discussed.

The cost of her parents' separation to Pamela is subtly revealed in the second half of *All Is Forgiven*, since although her stepfather André (Pascal Bongard) is depicted as an understanding man used to covering for Annette's inability to discuss her first marriage (it is André who mediates between Pamela and Victor's sister Martine (Carole Franck) about bringing daughter and father together again), Pamela also has a stepbrother and a half-brother to contend with. In conversation with Martine about her changed circumstances, Pamela admits to much affection for her 'obnoxious' little half-brother Lou (the son of André and Annette), but reports 'outright war' with her stepbrother Gaspard (André's son from his first marriage), who is the same age as her. Tension between Pamela and Annette about the past also becomes evident during the period in which Victor and Pamela are remaking acquaintance: Pamela refuses to join the family supper one evening, staying curled up on her bed in silence, then, when Annette phones her daughter to suggest they have lunch together the next day, Pamela declines, preferring the company of her schoolfriends.

The larger issue hanging over *All Is Forgiven*, forgiveness, is never mentioned or discussed in the second half of the film. As Jean-Marc Lalanne suggests, 'Pamela has no score to settle with her volatile father. He reappears and she opens her arms to him. Resentment does circulate in the film, but does not affect its main character. Its site is the film itself . . .'.[4] The words of the film's title seem to refer to Victor's behaviour during its first half, and sound spoken, but is their speaker Pamela? (it cannot be Annette, who never shows any inclination to discuss her separation from Victor, despite having given Pamela a minimal account of it that included Victor's mental illness). For Pamela, Victor has nothing to atone for. He does want to explain the past to her, however, unlike

Annette, and does so over dinner, furthering a kind of rewriting of the past that begins in Martine's initial meeting with Pamela, when she corrects the teenager's impression (supplied by Annette) that it was Victor who 'disappeared from circulation' when they separated. As the viewer knows, it was actually Annette who took Pamela away from her father, albeit in circumstances where he was unable to care for either of them. The minimal account of the past with which Annette has supplied her daughter misrepresented this central fact, and as Lalanne remarks: 'In a completely unexpected and almost unformulated fashion, *All Is Forgiven* does not forgive the mother for not having forgiven.'[5] Lalanne's observation that at Victor's funeral, the penultimate scene of the film, Annette is holding a rose she never places on Victor's coffin or throws into the grave, encapsulates her inability to forgive her ex-husband, an inability the film itself seems to want to make good. As one reviewer of *All Is Forgiven* says in an article entitled 'Family lives' [*Vies de famille*], family, filiation and separation are the issues at the heart of the film,[6] and the brief reacquaintance that Victor and Pamela are able to make before his early death allows for a degree of transmission from father to daughter, in the form of Victor's love of literature and poetry, such as the verse by German Romantic poet Joseph von Eichendorff he includes in his last letter to Pamela. The *fracture familiale* that marks *All Is Forgiven* will continue to mark the *famille recomposée* of Annette, André and their three children, in the form of the silence between Pamela and her mother about the past. It is repaired to a degree, however, by the short relationship Victor and his daughter enjoy when he and Martine are finally able to track Annette down after she has very effectively avoided all contact with them for years, and prevented any between Pamela and her father.

As with *All Is Forgiven*, the title of *Father of My Children* is voiced, this time in a voice only attributable to one character – Sylvia, the wife then widow of Grégoire Canvel. As Lalanne remarks of this film, this is odd in itself, since Sylvia is not a privileged protagonist of the film, even if she becomes more of one in its second half, along with eldest daughter Clémence.[7] In its first half, the Canvel family is happy and loving, despite the growing tension around Grégoire's work and how it takes him away from them, a source of conflict on the holiday to Italy when Sylvia finds him on the phone to the office despite an agreement that he leave his work at home. A counterpoint to the tension between Grégoire's work and his family life, however, is that his film company is a kind of second family, in which he depends hugely on his production director Bérénice (Dominique Frot) and production assistant Valérie (Sandrine Dumas) as well as on an accountant, a secretary and an intern, all of whom hold him in great esteem and affection. After his suicide, his Moon Films 'family' mourns in the same way as his wife and daughters, if not as intensely.

Grégoire's suicide shocks and stuns his family, his Moon Films colleagues and his wide circle of friends and acquaintances. Hansen-Løve elects to show Sylvia's grief first, as she meets Grégoire's colleague and friend Serge (Eric Elmosnino) on one of Paris's vast, echoey station concourses, then cuts to a scene at the family's flat where middle daughter Valentine (Alice Gautier) shares her tearful, angry reaction with Serge, who has told her she must think of her mother and sisters at this awful time; Grégoire did not think of them when taking his own life, she insists. If Valentine's reaction to Grégoire's death is the first to be articulated, Clémence's reaction seems the most profound, as she weeps on numerous occasions in the second half of the film. A rift opens up between Clémence and Sylvia after the former hears café gossip about Grégoire having had a 'double life' and a son he kept hidden who would be Clémence's half-brother: Clémence verifies this by reading letters written to Grégoire by his first wife years before, and then challenges Sylvia about the matter, getting the response that Grégoire did not abandon his son Moune, who was raised by his mother when the couple separated. Unconvinced or just too curious, Clémence contacts Grégoire's first wife Isabelle (Valérie Lang) and goes to visit her, but discovers that Moune, now an adult and married with a baby of his own, lives elsewhere in France and had little to no contact with his father. Isabelle, for her part, bears Grégoire no ill-will about their divorce and never saw him – so despite discovering the existence of a first wife and half-brother, Clémence uncovers nothing that will affect her present and future family life. The most striking thing about the depiction of family in the second half of *Father of My Children* is perhaps not how the Canvels adjust to Grégoire's absence or the family's detachment from the French film-making community brought about by the liquidation of Moon Films, but that Hansen-Løve elects not to show Grégoire's funeral (referred to only once, in the conversation between Clémence and Isabelle, when Clémence asks if Moune attended, which he did not). By omitting a funeral scene, Hansen-Løve's focus on the entirely private grief of Sylvia and her daughters is revealed, with the sorrow of the employees of Moon Films standing in for the public reaction to an unanticipated suicide (Figure 1.2).

It is a period of grieving for Grégoire rather than the complete process we follow in the second half of *Father of My Children*, as Clémence is still in tears when mother and daughters leave Paris

Figure 1.2 Mourning Grégoire at the Chapelle des Templiers, *Father of My Children*

for a holiday at the end of the film. The family is far from united about its future, since Sylvia has mentioned possibly returning to Italy to live, an idea Clémence and Valentine counter vigorously, but now that the always likely liquidation of Moon Films has been confirmed, a period of choices about the future is opening up. *Father of My Children* also continues the theme of filiation and transmission at the centre of *All Is Forgiven*'s focus on a father-daughter relationship, and this is picked up by Clémence's new friendship with Arthur Malkavian (Igor Hansen-Løve), an aspiring director her father had started to support but not had time actually to sign up – the real-life situation Hansen-Løve herself was in vis-à-vis Humbert Balsan when the producer took his own life in 2005. (The actor cast as Arthur Malkavian, Igor Hansen-Løve, is a cousin of the director.) The title of the script Malkavian has written and shows to Clémence is *Families of Chance* [*Les familles du hasard*], which resonates strongly with Moon Films as a kind of additional family to Grégoire, one becoming connected to his 'real' (legal) family through Malkavian's relationship with Clémence. By insisting that the sense of family extends beyond legal and biological relationships and by casting her cousin in the role indicating this, Hansen-Løve both highlights the proximity between relationships of filiation and affiliation and 'signs' this concern as one that is important to her.

Fractures of time and place in *Things to Come* and *Maya*

In *Things to Come*, the third of Hansen-Løve's dramas of family crisis, the separation of Heinz and Nathalie after twenty-five years of marriage is sudden and unanticipated, at least by Nathalie. The viewer is forewarned in unexpected fashion when the couple's daughter Chloé (Sarah Le Picard) surprises her father coming out of his workplace in order to confront him with the knowledge (shared by her brother Johann (Solal Forte)) that he is being unfaithful to their mother. Heinz's reaction, which is not to deny the fact and to respond to his children's request that he choose between the two women with a intellectual's quick nod of acknowledgement, does more to establish his character – he is a Kantian moral philosopher – than any other scene. When Heinz announces to Nathalie shortly afterwards that he is leaving, it is no surprise that he has been able to take his decision quickly, equipped as he is with a raft of moral principles derived from Enlightenment thought. The way in which his children compel him to choose is another indication that the family is a highly educated, middle-class one, even if making Heinz do this is not obviously a wise course of action.

Given that Chloé and Johann are already adults when their parents separate (though Johann barely), the fracture effected in *Things to Come*'s family does not set children's lives on a different course as it does in *All Is Forgiven* and *Father of My Children*. It affects Nathalie far more than the family's other members, though even for her, much remains the same, since she continues to teach and to live in the same roomy, comfortable apartment. For Nathalie, the sudden break-up of her marriage is above all a break with her own past, particularly with the holiday home in Brittany to which many memories of raising her children are attached. When she assures her former pupil Fabien that she is adjusting 'very well' to her new single status, the one matter that brings tears to her eyes is the loss of her connection to this home, because of the place memories it holds. Of course, Nathalie has also lost the main person with whom she is likely to reminisce about family occasions such as the visit to Chateaubriand's tomb seen in *Things to Come*'s opening scene, but (perhaps because she still has her children to talk to about these), it is the break with her own past that really hurts. Her memories of raising Chloé and Johann with Heinz will now no longer be stimulated, and despite having her own recall and probably some photographs to rely upon, she is deprived of an experiential reconnection with the place she most associates with being a mother.

The family is not as prominent a theme of *Maya* as it is of *All Is Forgiven*, *Father of My Children* and *Things to Come*, but might well be termed the main secondary theme of the film, firstly because it is the fact of having inherited a house in Goa from his maternal grandfather that allows Gabriel to be in India at all, and secondly, because an additional motive for his visit is to meet up with his mother in Mumbai. Gabriel's mother left his father for another man when he was seven, then remarried and remained in India, while his father, a diplomat, travelled and brought Gabriel up in a variety of locations. Gabriel's connection to India is not only through his childhood, his mother, and the house, however, because his godfather Monty (Pathy Aiyar) owns and runs the Nilaya hotel close to the inherited home he is clearing out and refurnishing. Maya (Aarshi Bannerjee), whom Gabriel meets on the way to the Nilaya for the first time, is Monty's daughter, and the Nilaya functions as a sort of family home in the film's story – for example, Gabriel spends Christmas there when he returns to India two months after breaking off the relationship he and Maya have just started. Monty's hospitality and kindness towards Gabriel – when Gabriel is knocked off his moped and the bike written off as he rides back from the beach one night Monty insists he stay in the hotel's best room for a night or two – is thoroughly familial.

Gabriel's meeting with his mother occurs at the end of a trip across India that he evidently wants to be a further part of the healing process behind his visit, and his expectations of it may be higher than he indicates beforehand. This is the first time he has seen her for many years (exactly how many is unclear), and in their initial exchanges Johanna reproaches him for not answering the messages she sent when he was liberated from captivity in Syria, and for never being available to meet on the occasions she has visited Paris in the last ten years – perhaps because he was away working, she surmises, but perhaps because he was avoiding her. (Gabriel does not answer this question.) Johanna works for an NGO concerned to address the effects of poverty on street children, and although her and Gabriel's conversation touches on family matters, it turns mainly around the very different convictions driving their respective working lives – Johanna does not agree with Gabriel's reasoning about the reporting he does in war-torn countries (particularly Syria) being necessary, and is bitterly opposed to French state funds changing hands to liberate hostages such as himself, when they are so urgently needed for humanitarian aid. She also reproaches him for giving more importance to his professional ethics than to his personal safety and the concern his family has for him: he cannot know what it was like for her during his recent period of captivity, she insists (a charge Gabriel does not answer). The brevity of the meeting between mother and son and the disconsolate mood it seems to put him in convey that it is a disappointment to Gabriel. (His mother, meanwhile, weeps bitterly as she drives away, indicating a depth of feeling about the distance – literal and emotional – between her and Gabriel that she did not articulate during their meeting.) The only person in whom Gabriel confides about this first re-encounter with his mother for many years is Maya, during a boat trip with Monty, his wife Sigrid and friends of theirs shortly after he returns to Goa. When Maya asks him whether he saw his mother as he intended, and what came of the meeting, he replies almost laconically that 'starting again' is not possible, and that 'she has her life. She doesn't need me'.

A later episode of *Maya* sheds further light on Gabriel's feelings about the unrepaired connection with his mother. This is the trip to Agonda that Gabriel and Maya take because his mother gave this place name to the house he has now inherited: he seems to be hoping that some significance attaching to the place will be revealed to him if he visits. In the event, he and Maya swim from Agonda's beach, but as they lie side by side afterwards, Gabriel suddenly says 'It's just another beach' – one of hundreds of idyllic sunbathing and swimming locations Goa has to offer. It is as if he takes cognisance at this moment that there may be no elusive meaning to his mother's choice of Agonda as a house name, and that he has been chasing rainbows by expecting it to deliver one, even if the name is linked to a house he treasures.

Not only does Gabriel's visit to Mumbai fail to help him make the hoped-for reconnection with his mother, but the associated connection that the house provides with his Indian childhood, as the site of many treasured memories, is also brutally severed. Several scenes in the first half of *Maya* show Gabriel at work renovating the house, and its link to childhood and family is emphasised by the friendship he strikes up with three local children, Kamod, Voappa and Nagma, who play in his garden and in the neighbourhood, and through whose parents he finds new furniture for the house. When Gabriel returns from a beach café to find the house in flames and a fire engine arriving just in front of him, Voappa comforts an evidently distressed Gabriel by standing with him outside, and when Gabriel returns to India at Christmas but cannot find Maya in her room at the Nilaya hotel, he immediately takes presents to all three children, who are delighted with the games. Play, whether it is the football he plays with the children or the 'Diabolo' game in one of his presents (which he starts teaching them in a very fatherly fashion), both denotes and connotes the childhood Gabriel seems to be trying to get in touch with, a childhood which is in a way also figured by Maya's being on the brink of adulthood but still treated extremely protectively by her father and stepmother.

Liquid society, precariousness, ethics and film

The postmodern sociology of Bauman's *Liquid Modernity* and *Liquid Love*, on which I drew above to contextualise Hansen-Løve's registration of the shifting, provisional character of social and familial relationships in contemporary Western societies,[8] has much in common with recent ethical writings about precarity – the vulnerable insecurity characterising millions of lives in the world's conflict-ridden twenty-first-century societies, as well as in developed and peaceful Western nations. One of the first philosophers to develop the ethical dimension(s) of precarity and precariousness was Judith Butler, starting with her book *Precarious Life: The Powers of Mourning and Violence* (2004),[9] since which she has published a series of books that blend ethical thinking with political theory and moral philosophy.[10] In 'Precarious Lives: On Girls in Mia Hansen-Løve and Others' (Wilson 2012), film commentator Emma Wilson brings Hansen-Løve's first two feature films into dialogue with Butler's *Giving an Account of Oneself* (2005), which followed the publication of *Precarious Life* and in which Butler explores some fundamental questions about self-knowledge, ethics and responsibility by drawing eclectically on the work of Adorno, Levinas, Foucault and Nietzsche. In this penultimate section of Chapter 1, I shall open discussion of the guiding thread of ethics that will run through Chapters 2, 3 and 6 - by bringing Wilson's Butler-inspired commentary on *All Is Forgiven* together with Butler's own writings on precarity and precariousness.

An engagement with film and visual media is promised by Butler in the preface to *Precarious Life* when she says of Levinas, 'Through a cultural transposition of his philosophy, it is possible to see how dominant forms of representation can and must be disrupted for something about the precariousness of life to be apprehended' (Butler 2004: xviii).[11] In 'Peace and Proximity', one of Levinas's commentaries on how the face – his figure for the ethical demand made on me by the other – 'is not exclusively a human face' (2004: 133), he uses the term precariousness explicitly, and Butler glosses this passage closely in the fifth, eponymous essay of *Precarious Life*, as follows:

> Levinas appends the following lines, which do not quite accomplish the sentence form: 'The face as the extreme precariousness of the other. Peace as awakeness to the precariousness of the other' (167). Both statements are similes, and they both avoid the verb, especially the copula. They do not say that the face *is* that precariousness, or that peace *is* the mode of being awake to an Other's precariousness. Both phrases are substitutions that refuse any commitment to the order of being. Levinas tells us, in fact, that 'humanity is a rupture of being'. (Butler 2004: 134)

Here Butler draws attention to how Levinas's remarks about the face perform the suspension and rupture of the order of being that the concept describes, after which she sums up her interpretation of Levinas by writing 'To respond to the face, to understand its meaning, means to be awake to what is precarious in another life, or, rather, the precariousness of life itself' (Butler 2004: 134).

Wilson's focus in 'Precarious Lives' is not exactly the precariousness of life itself (and therefore Levinasian ethics); it is, rather, the precariousness of subject formation – the shifting identities of girls in photography and film, including the adolescent Pamela of *All Is Forgiven*, and Valentine, the middle daughter of *Father of My Children*'s Canvel family. (Valentine is distinctly younger than Pamela, pubescent rather than on the verge of adulthood.) Wilson, affirming that Hansen-Løve's films 'ask what it is to be a subject, how far subjectivity can embrace or encompass those parts of our selves and our family history which remain opaque to us' (Wilson 2012: 278), wishes to draw on Butler's *Giving an Account of Oneself* to '[look] at the ways in which moving image representations can offer an approach to the girl subject as always in part opaque to herself, as always shifting, precarious, unfixed and unknowable' (2012: 273). In a sensitive and beautiful extended commentary on the scene in *All Is Forgiven* where Pamela and her friend Judith travel home on the overhead metro from Pamela's first re-encounter with Victor since her childhood, Wilson points to how Hansen-Løve's shots evoke 'the perception and feeling of Pamela, yet also leave us outside her direct range of emotion' (2012: 282). There is no dialogue in this scene, in which framing and light – 'radiant light, golden from the metro window' (2012: 282) instead work to convey Pamela's subjectivity during her silent absorption in thought. In Wilson's reading of the girls' metro journey, Hansen-Løve is pursuing a 'focus on passage and intermittent vision' (2012: 282), as the speed of the train and successive indistinct shots of what the girls see through its smeared and graffiti-daubed glass 'remind[s] us of its surface and substance separating Pamela from this passing world' (2012: 282). Wilson's account of how viewers of this scene are emotionally involved in Pamela's thoughtfulness and yet obliged by Hansen-Løve's cinematography to remain ignorant of what Pamela is thinking and feeling is preceded by a parallel and equally beautifully written commentary on the swim taken by Valentine during the family holiday in Italy in *Father of My Children*, of which Wilson finds that the film:

> makes me understand [. . .] the way in which knowledge of the other is always ungrounded, is always only projective, that our apprehension of another's subjectivity is the more acute, the more ethical in Butler's terms, the more we acknowledge what we cannot know of her experience and indeed what we cannot know of ourselves. (Wilson 2012: 282)

Seeking to 'think through responsibility and accountability' by looking at 'this interaction between precariousness and agency' (Wilson 2012: 279), Butler asks if 'the postulation of a subject [. . .] whose conditions of emergence can never fully be accounted for, undermine[s] the possibility of responsibility and, in particular, of giving an account of oneself?' (Butler 2005: 10). Butler argues that understanding 'the implications of the opacity of the subject' (Wilson 2012: 279) is crucial to developing 'a theory of subject formation that acknowledges the limits of self-knowledge' (Butler 2005: 19) and 'can serve a conception of ethics and, indeed, responsibility' (2005: 19). Wilson claims that the way in which Hansen-Løve represents 'the precariousness of her girls' lives, places emphasis on the binding of lives in relational networks whose meanings remain in part irrecoverable, opaque' (Wilson 2012: 279), and although I observe some sleight of hand in the way Wilson employs the concept of precariousness, which, as noted above, she applies to subject formation rather than life itself (she should perhaps not claim that Hansen-Løve represents her girls' lives as precarious when her argument relates predominantly to their subjectivities), her conclusion – that Hansen-Løve's 'extraordinarily sensitive, imaginative and attentive' film-making 'draws us to appreciate all that we cannot see and know of others' (2012: 279) – is finely crafted and utterly convincing.

Conclusion: girlhood and the ethics of
fracture familiale

Wilson had written widely about the representation of children
(particularly girls) in European film before discussing Hansen-
Løve's first two films in 'Precarious Lives',[12] but she is not the
only commentator to have focused on this aspect of Hansen-
Løve's work: Fiona Handyside explores *Goodbye First Love*
alongside Céline Sciamma's *Waterlilies*, two of a number of recent
French films that dramatise adolescent girlhood, in the chapter
she contributes to her co-edited book *International Cinema
and the Girl: Local Issues, Transnational Contexts* (Handyside
2016).[13] Going so far as to designate Sciamma and Hansen-Løve
themselves as girls,[14] a labelling one feels the directors might
object to, Handyside observes how both *Waterlilies* and *Goodbye
First Love* 'pay close attention to the inception of sexual feelings,
and their impact on the senses' (2016: 122), and through
soundscape and film form, 'create a politics of emotions, of affect,
that communicates how it feels to be a girl in a society that still
treats male and female sexual desire very differently despite the
legal and social equality of men and women' (122). Handyside's
idea that the French cinematic landscape is 'uniquely suited to'
a 'Girls' Cinema' (2016: 214) is highly convincing and applies
well to *All Is Forgiven, Father of My Children* and *Goodbye First
Love*: the French film industry has indeed had 'an industrial bias
toward the young from the days of the New Wave' (2016: 214),
and it is fascinating how in recent years, women directors such as
Sciamma and Hansen-Løve have been able to take advantage of
this bias to convey hitherto unrepresented aspects of girls' subjectivities. Handyside and Wilson are the two Anglophone critics
who have done the most to bring out the novelty, sensitivity and
imaginativeness of Hansen-Løve's representations of girls aged
between six and eighteen (or twenty-three/four if we consider
Camille still to be on the threshold of womanhood at the end of
Goodbye First Love), and the territory they have explored is a rich
and fertile one.

Where *fracture familiale* is concerned, the importance of young female characters to *All Is Forgiven*, *Father of My Children* and *Goodbye First Love* (three films that Hansen-Løve herself acknowledges form a loose trilogy on this account) is extremely telling, because it signals an ethical openness to modifiability and the future. The way Western women's lives – some women's lives – have changed in what we may term the postmodern era (from the 1960s to the present) is so as to accommodate an enormously increased diversity: the traditional 'wife and mother' role still exists, but no longer dominates, and adolescent girls face a far wider range of additional possible life-paths than they did up to the 1950s, including forging a career independently, living in a stable relationship or marriage without children, and raising children with another woman. The greater freedom and uncertainty of this expanded range of life-paths has implications for the future of the family at a time when it has already changed, almost beyond recognition, over quite a short period of time. Hansen-Løve's acute awareness of the rifts and difficulties in family lives associated with liquid modernity and liquid love is testament to the thoroughgoing contemporaneity of her filmmaking.

Notes

All translations, unless otherwise stated, are the author's own.

1 Blanchard et al. (2006).
2 Recent marriage and divorce rates in France can be seen at <https://www.insee.fr/fr/statistiques/3303338?sommaire=3353488> (last accessed 2 March 2020). For those across the EU, go to <https://ec.europa.eu/eurostat> and select the 'Population and social conditions' theme: typing in 'Crude marriage rate and crude divorce rate' will bring up the relevant datasets (last accessed 20 August 2020).
3 See Edith Turner (2012).
4 *Les Inrockuptibles,* 26 September 2007.
5 Ibid.
6 E.H., 'Vies de familles' in *Les Echos,* 1 October 2007.
7 Jean-Marc Lalanne, '*Le Père de mes enfants,* un portrait sensible et touchant', *Les Inrockuptibles,* 16 December 2009.

8 Despite the prevalence of broken families in Hansen-Løve's films, there are instances of togetherness and parental devotion that go against this fragility of family relations: Natalie, Chloé and Johann's Christmas Eve meal in the final scene of *Things to Come* is an example of the former, and the way Paul's mother stands by him when he crashes out of his DJ-ing career is perhaps the best instance of the latter. (Paul has borrowed money from his mother that he has not repaid and has not admitted to his longstanding drug problem, but she accepts both these failings.)

9 Strictly speaking, Butler first disclosed an interest in ethics in a much-cited interview called 'Politics, Power and Ethics: a Discussion between Judith Butler and William Connolly' (2000a) and an essay from the same year, 'Ethical Ambivalence', in Garber et al. (2000), pp. 15–28.

10 Judith Butler, *Giving an Account of Oneself* (2005); *Frames of War: When Is Life Grievable?* (2010); *Parting Ways: Jewishness and the Critique of Zionism* (2012); *Senses of the Subject* (2015).

11 To date, only a few philosophically inclined film critics have pursued connections between Butler's later work on ethics and visual culture, such as Nikolaj Lübecker in Section 2.2 of *The Feel-Bad Film* (2015), who draws on *Giving an Account of Oneself* and *Frames of War* (79–83), and Casey Ryan Kelly, who considers precarity in relation to the horror genre in '*It Follows*: precarity, thanatopolitics, and the ambient horror film' (2017), 234–49.

12 See Wilson (2003, 2005, 2006, 2007).

13 Handyside (2016), pp. 121–33.

14 'While clearly they have both reached their majority and are therefore legally adult, Sciamma and Hansen-Løve can be labeled girls for two reasons' (Handyside 2016: 124).

2

Vulnerable people

Vulnerability has been an important concept in a lot of recent ethical theory, having been addressed by philosophers as well-known as Julia Kristeva and Judith Butler. Kristeva's essay on vulnerability 'Liberty, Equality, Fraternity . . . and Vulnerability' (2010) suggested that the concept should be added to France's 'Liberty, Equality, Fraternity' motto of humanist Enlightenment values, and the blend of ethical thinking with political theory and moral philosophy in Butler's recent writings that was set out at the end of Chapter 1 draws particularly on vulnerability as well as precariousness. Another philosopher to have written extensively on vulnerability and vulnerable subjectivity is feminist legal theorist Martha Fineman: her 2004 book *The Autonomy Myth: A Theory of Dependency* sought to expose the particularly American myth, enshrined in law across the US, that citizens can and should be autonomous, and in some extremely influential articles that followed the book Fineman develops vulnerability as an alternative paradigm to autonomy. According to Fineman (2008: 1) 'vulnerability is – and should be understood to be – universal and constant, inherent in the human condition'. As a legal theorist, her purpose in developing what she calls 'vulnerability analysis' is 'to argue for a more responsive state and a more egalitarian society' (2008: 1). However, the importance of her approach for my purposes is that she 'want[s] to claim the term "vulnerable" for its potential in describing a universal, inevitable, enduring aspect of the human condition' (2008: 8) rather than for its 'limited and negative' associations of 'victimhood, deprivation, dependency, or pathology' when it qualifies 'groups of fledgling or stigmatized subjects [that are] designated as "populations"' (2008: 5). Fineman's 'vulnerability approach' to subjectivity 'both expands upon and complements earlier work I have done in theorizing dependency' (2008: 9), and secondly, and importantly for its consonance with other feminist-philosophical enquiries into this topic, 'should be understood as arising from our embodiment' (2008: 9).

A vulnerability 'arising from our embodiment' also accurately describes Butler's development of the term in 'Precarious Life' (2004) and in *Frames of War: When is Life Grievable?* (2010). She does however mention vulnerability several years earlier in the essay 'Ethical Ambivalence' (Butler 2000b: 25), in a commentary on the Levinasian subject, where she describes any claim for the self-identity of the subject as 'an act of irresponsibility, an effort to close off one's fundamental *vulnerability* to the Other, the primary accusation that the Other bears' (2000b: 25, my emphasis). As Moya Lloyd (2008) emphasises, 'Ethical Ambivalence' and the writings that followed the events of 11/9/2001 in New York highlight that, for Butler, vulnerability is vulnerability to violence: she sees the US's exposure to the world as vulnerable by the 11/9/2001 events as an opportunity 'to reflect on the relation between human vulnerability and violence'; and to consider 'what, politically, might be made of grief besides a cry for war' (Lloyd 2008: 93). Lloyd summarises, 'in short, this is an ethics, indeed a potentially global ethics, which issues out of a common human experience of vulnerability, and particularly vulnerability to violence' (2008: 92). It is because vulnerability as conceptualised by Butler is vulnerability to violence[1] that I have expounded it here alongside Fineman's theory of the vulnerable subject, in which loss, grief and (potential or actual) violence do not figure significantly, since this difference will be important later in my analysis.

Many of the characters that Mia Hansen-Løve has brought to the screen have vulnerability as a striking characteristic: in *All Is Forgiven*, the intelligent and well-read Victor (Paul Blain) is incapable of holding down a job that would support his wife and child as well as himself, instead spending his days writing, walking around the city and taking drugs. Grégoire Canvel (Louis-do de Lencquesaing) of *Father of My Children* has been an admired film producer, husband of Sylvia (Chiara Caselli) and father to their three daughters for many years, but despite professional success has failed to face up to his inadequate financial management of his company Moon Films for this entire period. Paul Vallée (Félix de Givry), the DJ protagonist of *Eden*, resembles Grégoire in his incapacity to face up to diminishing professional success, which leads to a temporary breakdown resembling Victor's. Vulnerable masculinity – in the first two instances flawed fatherhood (and it is significant, too, that *Eden*'s Paul only finally gives up music when he learns that his girlfriend from the DJ-ing years aborted their child) – is thus a hallmark of three of Hansen-Løve's first four films. (The fifth, *Things to Come*, will not feature in this chapter because neither of its significant male characters exhibit vulnerability – husband Heinz [André Marcon] is the unfaithful husband who makes a seemingly smooth transition to a life with his new partner when compelled by his children to choose between their mother and her, and Fabien [Roman Kolinka] is an entirely healthy young man emotionally, morally and intellectually.) There is at least one vulnerable woman in Hansen-Løve's films, Camille (Lola Créton) of *Goodbye First Love*, a film whose men, like those of *Things to Come*, successfully manage any vulnerabilities that are dogging them. Camille attempts suicide when the overwhelming passion of her teenage relationship with Sullivan (Sebastian Urzendowsky) does not stop him leaving her to travel for an extended period. Vulnerable masculinity is again to the fore in Hansen-Løve's sixth film *Maya* (2018), whose central character Gabriel (Roman Kolinka) takes time out to recover from his months of captivity as a hostage in Syria.[2]

Fragile life in *All Is Forgiven*

Of all Hansen-Løve's leading protagonists, wayward husband Victor is the most obviously psychologically vulnerable, arguably even in the pathological sense used as a category by some writers about vulnerability. Victor's consumption of alcohol early in the day is the first indication of his fragile disposition, followed by drug-taking, as a carefully paced scene observes him make an excuse about running an errand in order to leave Annette (Marie-Christine Friedrich) and Pamela (Victoire Rousseau) during their afternoon out in Vienna and meet a contact from whom he can score. Barely any words are exchanged during this risky rendez-vous, about which Victor predictably says nothing to Annette. In Paris, in due course, we see Victor talk to a sympathetic medical practitioner who grants his first request for a prescription but later refuses to renew it, because Victor is not even trying to work at autonomous paid employment and by not respecting their contract regarding his dependency on drugs, is exploiting the doctor's goodwill. A short episode in the first, Vienna-based chapter of *All Is Forgiven* gives symbolic expression to Victor's psychological and physical problems with dependency: at the end of the same afternoon on which Victor abandons his wife and daughter to meet his drug-dealer, the family returns home via a bridge over the Danube from which Victor points out the Reichsbrücke – a reconstructed bridge whose original structure collapsed when it was a hundred years old, in 1976. His aim is to tease and light-heartedly scare Pamela by suggesting that the bridge's collapse was a modern urban disaster, when in fact, he quickly admits, it happened at night and only one life was lost. But in her momentary alarm about the fragility of bridges, Pamela calls out to her mother, who reassures her in German that bridges are built out of strong materials and do not collapse easily. As she goes on to further reassure her daughter that 'bridges are indestructible', walking away and ahead of Victor as she does so, the camera remains on him as he impassively listens to his wife's dismissal of his parable about unpredictable and inexplicable fragility. It is an issue that evidently concerns him, and one she does not understand.

Insights into Victor's vulnerability that demonstrate the pressure of (hetero)normative ideals of masculinity are offered in a dialogue with his sister Martine (Carole Franck) shortly after the family's return to Paris. Despite having previously taught literature at university level and privately, and coming under pressure from his wife to bring in an income, Victor is no longer willing to take a higher teaching qualification or earn his living in this way: his idea of how to spend his time is to work (intellectual work comprising reading and writing) in the mornings, to occupy his afternoons with *flâneur*-style walks around the city, and to take drugs in the evenings. Although she laughs at the apparently unconcerned attitude and defence of this lifestyle, both produced by the unbearable anxiety Victor also describes, Martine, who will later offer her brother unstinting support in the process of reuniting with Pamela, advises him practically that he should seek out her company or that of friends when he needs to talk, rather than expecting the understanding of his conventional young wife. Victor's breakdown occurs when, after he and Annette separate, he takes further risks with his health by becoming involved with a heroin addict called Gisèle (Olivia Ross) via a drug-dealer friend called Zoltan (Wieland Amand), moves in with her at Zoltan's, and starts to share her heroin habit. The overdose Gisèle takes one night while Victor is asleep evidently shakes him to the core, as the scene of his panic at finding Gisèle's cold body cuts to one in a hospital ward where Annette is arriving to visit: Victor has been shocked into realising the extent of his dependency, and although he is able to leave his bed, he shuffles along like an old man (Figure 2.1). Although we meet a re-energised and healthier Victor in the second part of *All Is Forgiven*, explained by Martine to be much more at peace with himself than when he and Annette separated eleven years earlier, news of his death reaches Pamela (Constance Rousseau) at her

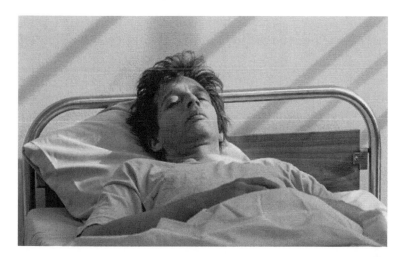

Figure 2.1 Victor in hospital, *All Is Forgiven*

step-grandfather Paul's (Claude Duneton) shortly afterwards. Just prior to the phone call that brings the news, a sequence of cross-cut shots of Victor and Pamela writing to one another and reading each other's letters culminates in a short scene of Victor in his Paris flat, alone but occupied writing, smoking a cigarette and drinking coffee. The window is open, the light bright, and he is listening to music, apparently contented, and more deeply so when he reclines on the bed to read a letter from his daughter. Nothing indicates his imminent death, due to a fragility or vulnerability as mysterious as that of the collapsed Reichsbrücke over the Danube with which he briefly alarmed the young Pamela years earlier.

Risk, denial and failure in *Father of My Children*

In the opening sequence of *Father of My Children*, a set of shots of Grégoire Canvel doing business on his mobile phone while walking to his car make him look every inch the debonair, successful film producer. Yet as Jean-Marc Lalanne (2009) points out, it is soon evident that Grégoire is a man whose time is running out: he is pulled over by the police for speeding as he approaches the second home his family visits at weekends, learns his licence has run out of points, and has it temporarily confiscated. This literal loss of autonomy exposes Grégoire's dependency on his family, but also subtly reveals, through his unawareness that a single additional infraction will lose him his driving licence, how he tends to take risks he simultaneously blocks out. A phone conversation with his production assistant Valérie (Sandrine Dumas) during the drive has already revealed that the director of one of his company's current productions, Stig Janson (Magne-Håvard Brekke), is overspending enormously by insisting on reshooting scenes he is unhappy with and by finding alternative locations, yet Grégoire, who replies that there is no point in acting on this, is entirely oblivious to the danger of the situation.

It is only after Grégoire's suicide, as his eldest daughter Clémence (Alice de Lencquesaing) discovers she has a half-brother from her father's first marriage, that Grégoire's past connects with his shocking decision and shows his vulnerabilities to be enduring: a letter to him from his first wife Isabelle (Valérie Lang) reveals that their son Moune began having minor behavioural problems when he first attended school. These worsened, leading her to forecast his turning into 'a sad man interested only in his sterile eccentricity', yet despite risking being submerged in debt Grégoire gave generously to Isabelle for Moune. In another letter written to Sylvia as he set up Moon Films in Paris, Grégoire describes the solitude and depression of his widowed father, who rarely left the house and seemed to have given up on life. Grégoire's comment about how his father's house suffered visibly from the absence of women is impossible not to understand in relation to the four women and girls of his own family, and his dependency on them for love, company and happiness – emotional stability, in short. Grégoire's personal and professional lives are fuelled by love and passion, and by indulging his admiration for directors he considers geniuses (a word he uses about Stig Janson) over many years, he has disregarded the financial consequences of his behaviour in a way that risks both his own business and the security and well-being of his family.

Several scenes leading up to Grégoire's suicide reveal the full extent of his denial of Moon Films' debts. When the company's bookkeeper Frédéric (Antoine Mathieu) reminds him that the lab that processes all their film stock is owed €1m plus interest, Grégoire simply suggests that it may help if he has lunch with the lab's new manager, and he is again far too relaxed in the offices of the Ciné-Credit bank where, after the cast and crew of Stig Janson's film *Saturn* cash pay cheques for a huge sum of money when the film is already way over budget, Grégoire is reminded that he is €4m in the red. Back at Moon Films' office, he fobs off Valérie's warning that the company is going under with vague appeals to the future. Shortly afterwards, Valérie deposits a post-it on his desk reading 'Your lawyer says to call', but although Grégoire checks his mobile phone, we do not see him do this, and a cut to the family's flat reveals that he has left the office unusually early, to Sylvia's surprise and concern. Grégoire's depression starts to become visible; his movements are slow and heavy, his attention turned in upon himself. At the office the next day he takes a siesta, before the action cuts to a darkened cinema where he is viewing rushes, and a text message flashes up telling him that the tax department is sending in bailiffs. When Grégoire meets Sylvia that evening on a bridge over the Seine near the Cinémathèque, where he is due to speak at a function, his first words are 'It's over . . . It's such a failure'. He does manage to drive to the office the next day, deal with some minor matters, and let Valérie know he is as up-to-date as her with the freezing of Moon Films' assets and seizing of the negatives of one film in production. However, after staring at his

Figure 2.2 Grégoire in his Moon Films office, *Father of My Children*

reflection in the blank screen of the laptop on his desk, he says he is going out to take some air, and leaves the office for the final time (Figure 2.2).

Failing fatherhood and postmodern French masculinities

These masculine protagonists of Hansen-Løve's first two films remain sympathetic characters despite their failings and risk-taking behaviour: Victor may not provide for Pamela financially for long, but he was never an unworthy ('*indigne*') father, as he tells her when re-explaining the family's past in order to correct her mother's mis-representations. Like Grégoire with younger daughters Valentine (Alice Gautier) and Billie (Manelle Driss), Victor plays with the young Pamela imaginatively and shows his affection for her both physically and verbally when they are reunited after time apart. In *Father of My Children*, when Clémence discovers that she has a half-brother from Grégoire's first marriage, she is ready to accuse him of having abandoned his first-born, but is corrected by her mother's account of how Grégoire's first marriage ended: finding fault with him as a father is not as straightforward as she imagined. But fatherhood is unquestionably a problem for Victor and Grégoire, whose dependency on their spouses and families is compounded by risk-taking behaviour that endangers those closest to them as well as themselves. This behaviour demonstrates a lack of agency over their vulnerabilities (Victor through lack of will, Grégoire through denial), when the daughters who depend on them, by virtue of their youth and legal status as minors, cannot exercise agency over the precarity their fathers create. For Hansen-Løve, it seems, risk-taking is a masculine behaviour that might itself be seen as a vulnerability, but above all exposes the inefficacy of agency in managing the vulnerabilities of others (dependents) as well as one's own. As we shall see shortly, in *Goodbye First Love*, *Eden* and *Maya*, fatherhood is a state that male protagonists Sullivan, Paul and Gabriel (all aged between nineteen and thirty-four) do not even aspire to: that Gabriel's ex-girlfriend Naomi (Judith Chemla) wanted a baby when he did not is a point he reminds her of when she but not he wants their relationship to resume after his return from Syria. Gabriel's dangerous occupation as a war reporter makes him a risk-taker like Victor and Grégoire, albeit of a more courageous kind, and he, Sullivan and Paul are in fact never in the same place for long enough to be suited to fatherhood, as the next two sections will detail.

The work of Lawrence R. Schehr in *French Post-Modern Masculinities* (2009) can help contextualise the increased vulnerability and decreased capacity shown by Hansen-Løve's inadequate and 'absent' male protagonists; in his book Schehr tackles head-on 'a changing hegemony in which heteronormativity and phallogocentrism have themselves perhaps finally come face-to-face with notions of their own mortality' (2009: 1). Schehr's thesis is both historical and relates particularly to representational art forms and media: 'as traditional notions of masculinity and male sexualities have been put into question in France, there have been representational reactions to, and incarnations of, changing masculinities in the post-modern world, and this, in a variety of genres' (2009: 1).

Although he acknowledges that in 'an analysis of the crisis in masculinity in the post-modern subject, any temporal beginning would be somewhat arbitrary' (2009: 8), Schehr argues that 'the most enduring and far-reaching effects' of France's 1968 events and associated cultural revolution 'were seen in the movements of liberation, particularly the women's movement and gay liberation, which were both repositionings of the sexual and the political' (2009: 8–9). Selecting 'AIDS and the Internet' as two particularly appropriate names for 'a turning point for this voyage toward new forms of masculinity' while admitting that others such as 'mobile phones, globalization, and GPS' would be equally suitable, Schehr argues that all these names are 'signs of the end of the independent subject in the nineteenth-century sense of the anonymous or invisible Baudelairean flâneur'. They are 'signs of the fact that the individual is never fully alone and never fully himself' (2009: 10): Schehr's masculinisation of the pronoun being fully justified by the fact that masculinity/ies are the object of his enquiry.

There have been manifold changes to French masculinities over the last third of the twentieth century and first part of the twenty-first, chartable first in the gay liberation movement and the AIDS crisis, and then in important legal changes to the family: in 1999 the PaCS or *pacte civil de solidarité* allowed civil union between two adults for the first time, anticipating the introduction of gay marriage (*le mariage pour tous*) in 2013. In the space of fifteen years, a radically altered legal framework transformed the types of interdependencies into which men could enter. Taking the view that the 'death of the author' written about by Roland Barthes and Michel Foucault at the end of the 1960s can with equal validity be termed 'the death of the subject', Schehr suggests that these changes 'could therefore be seen, in a perverse way, as the feminization of the male subject in a manner that defines the new masculinity as a visible, palpable, vulnerability' (Schehr 2009: 11). The texts in which he goes on to demonstrate this vulnerability are mainly literary and by exclusively male authors - Guillaume Dustan, Erik Rémès, Maurice G. Dantec, Fabrice Neaud (a graphic novelist), Nicolas Jones-Gorlin, Michel Houellebecq and Marc-Edouard

Nabe. The only filmmakers Schehr treats are Sébastien Lifshitz and the writing-directorial team of Olivier Ducastel and Jacques Martineau, both of whose films treat predominantly gay and transgender themes. Schehr's study is about the narrators and characters that people these writers' and filmmakers' texts, but not about their authors or authorship; therefore, his historical survey and theorisation of French postmodern masculinities is, I maintain, equally relevant to films made by a French female director between 2007 and 2018 as to the works he analyses in *French Post-Modern Masculinities*. Hansen-Løve's male characters are exclusively heterosexual, and it is arguable to what extent their vulnerabilities intersect with their sexual relationships with women, although interestingly, this is more obvious in the recent *Maya*. However, the range of observations collected in Schehr's very sexuality-focused theoretical and historical study can certainly usefully elucidate a cinema (Hansen-Løve's) in which men are more often vulnerable than not, and heteronormative masculine ideals therefore no longer hegemonic.

Life crises in *Eden* and *Goodbye First Love*

The character played by Roman Kolinka in *Eden*, Cyril (one of the group around DJ Paul Vallée), draws constantly and acts as illustrator for the artwork needs of Paul and Stan's (Hugo Conzelmann) duo *Cheers* and other musicians. For as long as he is in a relationship with his girlfriend Anaïs (Zita Hanrot) his life is stable, but when they split up he gets thrown out of a club night for fighting, after which he tells Paul how lucky he is to have Louise (Pauline Etienne), and confesses that living at night depresses him. He walks out of an initially very good-natured argument about the quality of Paul Verhoeven's film *Showgirls*, which he rubbishes, then refuses to come on *Cheers*'s US tour because of a work deadline and because he does not think he is needed by the group, none of whom notice how depressed he has become. When Paul hears from Stan, at the offices of the New York radio station Radio FG, that Cyril has taken his own life by throwing himself under a metro train, he exits from the broadcasting studio and weeps, and the action cuts back to Paris and Cyril's funeral, at which they admire the graphic novel *Le Chant de la Machine* he was struggling to complete as they left to go on tour.

Cyril's suicide is at least part of the reason that Paul splits up with Louise, his second serious girlfriend, as she is deeply affected by it, something Paul is unable or unwilling to deal with. Throughout his DJ-ing years, Paul borrows money from his mother (Arsinée Khanijan) without telling her that he has a cocaine habit, and has a string of relationships with women – the long-term one with Louise, followed by a much less stable one with Margot (Laura Smet), who is succeeded by Yasmin (Golshifteh Farahani), on whom Paul seems more practically dependent than previous girlfriends. After leaving Margot out of frustration at being strung along, but before meeting Yasmin, Paul goes to visit Louise, now in another relationship with two young children and living on France's north coast. In due course, Louise separates from the father of her children and returns to Paris to stay with her mother, a period during which she and Paul see one another and (as when he visited her *en famille*), he seems comfortable helping her out with the children. This rekindling of their relationship occurs not long after the first occasion on which Yasmin rescues Paul from danger, when he gets drunk at a commercially disastrous New Year's Eve party on a riverboat and almost goes overboard, evidently becoming desperate about his financial problems. But the trigger for his breakdown is learning, during what seems to be a springtime walk with Louise and her children in Paris's Luxembourg gardens, that she aborted their child without telling him during the DJ-ing years. Visibly shocked, Paul returns home immediately and is found by Yasmin not long afterwards collapsed on the floor of his flat and moaning 'stop the music'. Yasmin takes him to his mother's, and when he comes round, Paul confesses his cocaine addiction as well as the enormous debts his mother already knows about. So, although the crisis that causes Paul to turn his life around is due in large part to waning audiences at club nights and the consequent money problems, a new awareness of a missed opportunity of fatherhood is also a key factor.

The mode of vulnerability exhibited by Paul Vallée in *Eden* is to some extent gender-stereotypical, as a youth extended into one's mid-30s by a profession that allows a life without fixed routines is a life course more likely to be followed by men than women. And although Hansen-Løve individualises her characters' patterns of relationality extremely carefully, the same could be said about the crisis undergone by Camille in *Goodbye First Love*, which stems from the unusual earnestness with which she lives her passionate relationship with Sullivan (at nineteen, four years her senior). Early in the relationship she tells her mother that love is the only thing that matters to her, her 'reason for living', and while Sullivan is preparing the trip to South America that will separate them for at least a year, Camille (he reports to his mother) threatens to throw herself into the Seine if he leaves as planned. Sullivan is the source of meaning in Camille's life, and once he has departed, it is evident that none remains: by attending school and visiting the family's second home in the Ardèche with her parents rather than her lover, Camille is just going through the motions. Sullivan writes passionately to begin with, but when the letters peter out after a conclusive-sounding questioning of the 'reality' of their relationship (Sullivan says he feels as if he dreamt it), Camille takes the pins out of the map of South America on which she has charted his travels, removes the map from the wall, and swallows an overdose of pills taken from the family bathroom. For years afterwards she is unable to allow any other man to touch her, and even when she is fully recovered from the depression that led to her suicide attempt and in a relationship with Lorenz (Magne-Håvard Brekke), a chance meeting with Sullivan's mother on a bus presents her with an opportunity for contact she is unable to resist: she gives Selma (Özay Fecht) her mobile number, Sullivan sends her a text message not long afterwards, and the couple begin meeting regularly again, resuming their sexual relationship. Camille is in thrall to this passion, and takes increasing risks over where she and Sullivan meet – in a hotel room after she tells him she will sleep with him, then in a disused building Camille has access to via her architectural project, and then in the flat she now shares with Lorenz, who is working away from Paris at this time. Although she is finally thwarted by a train strike that prevents her from travelling to Marseille to spend a weekend with Sullivan, the resumption of their relationship literally comes closer and closer to home, indicating that her declaration to her mother at fifteen that love is her only reason for living is still governing her behaviour, an arguably self-destructive tendency she cannot resist, and perhaps one stereotypically found in adolescent and young women.

Sullivan does not suffer a life crisis on account of his and Camille's relationship, but behaves comparably to other Hansen-Løve male protagonists in the manner in which he ends it, on both occasions (while travelling in South America and in a letter sent to Camille's mother's home after the months during which the affair is resumed in adulthood). In the second letter, Sullivan says he is leaving Camille (again) because he does not know how to control his love for her, how to fit it into a life without a desire for a lasting relationship and children. (This is to judge by his reaction to a sketch of a man with a child Camille buys for him on their last meeting in Paris – he weeps, then forgets to take the sketch with him when he leaves the following morning.) Their love is stronger than passing time, he suggests, and he hopes they (although this must really only refer to him) will meet again later in life when they are better able to deal with it, a hollow-sounding if evidently sincere declaration. Although he does not say so, Sullivan's letter, like the one he wrote from South America years previously, reveals him to be incapable of the kind of relationship Camille wants and demonstrates herself suited to. And this seems to be because he needs autonomy in his personal life, in contrast to secure dependency: being single and having flings (*aventures*) is the life he describes to Camille when they first meet again in Paris (to her displeasure), whereas she seeks (and has found in Lorenz) stable mutual dependency.

Recovery time in *Maya*

The handsome, slender figure of Gabriel (Roman Kolinka) is constantly in the frame in *Maya*, and it is tempting to think that Hansen-Løve has cast him with his physique in mind, even if she has explained her choice as wanting to give a lead role to an actor who already had two admired performances to his credit in *Eden* and *Things to Come*. *Maya* opens on a mirror shot of Gabriel in the shower at the hotel at which he and Frédéric (Alex Descas) are staying before being flown back from the Middle East to Paris, and an enormous area of bruising from the violence he has been subjected to as a hostage is clearly visible on his back. When Gabriel emerges from the shower into the bedroom, his emaciation is apparent, confirmed at the hospital check-up a day or so later when his weight (he is 1.83m or 6ft tall) is recorded at 61 kilos or 9st 8lbs (far lower than before his captivity, judging by Gabriel's reaction). Physical vulnerability is therefore part of Gabriel's appearance and persona throughout *Maya*, and since he is lightly clad and spends a lot of time reclining on beds or walking on beaches and through touristic sites, we have ample opportunities to observe his frailty.

Whether Gabriel's condition following his ordeal in Syria is 'post-traumatic' is a question posed by some of *Maya*'s reviewers, as well as one put to him by the psychiatrist he sees at the Paris hospital straight after his return to France. This specialist in the effects of captivity asks him if he would describe his four months as a hostage as 'traumatising', to which Gabriel replies very precisely that that is not the term he would use. He passes a test of his ability to talk about the torture, beatings, and other psychologically violent aspects of his captivity, and opts not to take advantage of the course of psychotherapy on offer, saying that for him, action is more therapeutic than words (a telling statement from a reporter regarded by his colleague Frédéric as the more gifted of the two of them at writing). Since Gabriel does appear to recover fully from his Syrian ordeal in due course, this avoidance of psychiatrists and psychotherapy seems as much a deliberate aloofness from debates about talking therapies by Hansen-Løve as writer and director as anything else: even if Gabriel confides a few important facts about his childhood and family to Maya (Aarshi Bannerjee) during his months in India, he is certainly not someone to rely on language and narration to deal with feelings and difficult experiences, as he tells the Parisian psychiatrist. He displays no unusual psychological vulnerability, but vulnerability is relevant to *Maya* because the film is all about how we react to and recover from testing and violent experiences.

Vulnerability is also progressively played out in Gabriel's relationship with Maya,[3] in which he uses his professional commitment as a reason not to become involved, and when he does, is as absent as he is present. When Maya awakens alone after their first night together and has to go outside to locate him, he makes a rather feeble excuse about her looking so happy as she slept, and when he returns to India at Christmas, he leaves the morning after their reunion. Like Sullivan of *Goodbye First Love*, whom Hansen-Løve describes as possessing a fickleness [*quelque chose de fuyant*] that makes him 'elusive [*insaisissable*] from start to finish', Gabriel suffers from 'an inability to be present' [*une incapacité à être là*] (as quoted in Delorme 2011: 54), a type of masculine inadequacy that shapes the narrative of *Goodbye First Love*, *Eden* and *Maya*.

Reconfiguring male domination

In a 2015 essay entitled 'Pitiful Men, Instrumental Women: the Reconfiguration of Masculine Domination in Contemporary Popular French Cinema', feminist critic Geneviève Sellier examines a range of recent French films that feature vulnerable and/or inadequate male characters:

> Indeed, it seems that popular French cinema, compelled as a result of social developments to give up the possibility of delivering an unequivocal eulogy of a patriarchal,

virile masculinity (such as that embodied by Gabin in the 1960s, then Delon and Belmondo in the 1980s), has (provisionally?) constructed a fallback position that consists of highlighting masculine figures who are vulnerable, defective, disabled, pitiful, or neurotic, and with whom the spectator – especially the female spectator – is invited to empathize. The function of female characters is to relay this empathetic gaze through the fiction by acting as an antipathetic foil (bad mother, vindictive wife, manipulative mistress), which has the effect of making the insufficiencies of the male character seem more than excusable. *To find alternative configurations of gender, one unquestionably would need to look at less popular films, lower down in the box-office statistics.* (2015: 936–7, my emphasis)[4]

I argue that Hansen-Løve's critically highly successful but commercially quite averagely performing cinema offers exactly the sort of 'alternative configurations of gender' Sellier thinks might be found in 'less popular' films: she completes the conclusion from which the quotation above is taken by saying, 'even then, however, it is not certain that one would find at the other pole, in auteur cinema, representations that are any more finely attuned to the contradictory reality of male/female relations that pertain in contemporary France' (Sellier 2015: 937). Hansen-Løve's auteur cinema furnishes multiple scenarios of this 'contradictory reality of male/female relations'. There are no stereotypical bad mothers, vindictive wives and manipulative mistresses among the women associated with the male protagonists I have discussed, but a whole range of character types – cold bourgeoise Annette in *All Is Forgiven*, loving and long-suffering Sylvia in *Father of My Children*, the string of different women who have relationships with *Eden*'s Paul, and the beautiful and intelligent (if possibly rather innocent, on account of her youth) Maya. Hansen-Løve's films seem to be exploring the very contradictory reality of heterosexual gender relations to whose existence Sellier points: their vulnerable men, who are also 'failing', inadequate fathers or not fathers at all, point towards a de-patriarchalised or post-patriarchal society, which an account of subjectivity organised around dependency or interdependency may facilitate much more successfully than one that assumes or aspires to autonomy.

Vulnerabilisation of the subject

In proposing a concept of vulnerable subjectivity to replace the universal subject underpinning the liberal tradition of political philosophy, Fineman (2008) is targeting the notion of an autonomous, non-dependent subject that Western philosophy may usually have claimed to be gender-neutral, but whose masculinisation has been thoroughly unmasked and exposed by feminist scholarship:

> feminist scholars have scrutinized and criticized the ways in which dominant theory and popular politics idealize notions of independence, autonomy, and self-sufficiency that are empirically unrealistic and unrealizable. Feminist critics, specifically in bringing dependency and care work into light and under scrutiny, have offered a model of interdependence in which the liberal subject is enmeshed in a web of relationships and perceived as dependent upon them. (Fineman 2008: 11)

Fineman's work, which she has described as 'post-metaphysical', does not engage with the entire tradition of Western philosophy and the range of approaches to the autonomous subject taken by philosophers of ethics.[5] In targeting autonomy and replacing it with vulnerability, however, she draws attention to the importance of dependency and interdependence, highlighting the part that feminist philosophy has played in exposing that autonomy is not and never has been gender-neutral. In their introduction to *Vulnerability: New Essays in Ethics and Feminist Philosophy* (2014), Catriona Mackenzie, Wendy Rogers and Susan Dodds claim that there has been little systematic analysis of the concept of vulnerability ... despite its importance to debates about the ethics of care (Virginia Held, Eva Kittay), bioethics (UNESCO and the

European Commission's Basic Ethical Principles in Bioethics and Biolaw) and the interest Butler's work has sparked in 'the notion of vulnerability as an ontological condition of our humanity' (Mackenzie, Rogers and Dodds 2014: 1–2). Fineman, however, stated in 2008 that she has moved from the critique of autonomy and analysis of dependency to the development of vulnerability because it is 'a more encompassing concept', 'may ultimately prove more theoretically powerful', and can generate more 'politically potent analyses' (Fineman 2008: 11).

In considering whose approach to vulnerability can best account for the anxiety, proneness to addiction, denial, dependency on women, and emotional fickleness of the leading male characters of Hansen-Løve's films, Fineman's concept of the vulnerable subject seems better than the approach to vulnerability taken by Butler in her recent ethical and moral-philosophical writings. The Levinasian subject Butler brings into her thinking in these writings is utterly different from the autonomous and sovereign subject of ontologically grounded philosophies, since it is by reversing the priority of ontology over ethics that Levinas reconfigures ethics as a 'persecution' or originary vulnerability that precedes being. Butler can be said to be emphasising our lack of autonomy and dependency on others for our survival in the same way as Fineman does, but since the vulnerability Butler envisages is 'particularly vulnerability to violence' (Lloyd 2008: 92) and the threat of violence and any dynamics of vengeance (actual or potential) are entirely absent from the enmeshed, web-like dependency that characterises the social existence and emotional lives of Hansen-Løve's characters, Butler's approach offers less to an analysis of her films. The vulnerability of Hansen-Løve's leading protagonists takes different forms, while always relating to their intersubjective bonds with others, and affecting men distinctly more than women. Hansen-Løve's variously vulnerable men call for a contemporary philosophical approach to subjectivity that takes account of ongoing changes to Western masculinity and heterosexual gender relations, and Fineman's concept of the vulnerable subject offers just such an approach.

Notes

All translations, unless otherwise stated, are the author's own.

1   Vulnerability's relationship to violence is also explored in Maria Flood's '"The very worst things": violence and vulnerability in Djamila Sahraoui's *Yema* (2012)' (2018).

2   By addressing vulnerability primarily as it is seen in Hansen-Løve's male characters here, I am going against the grain of the Anglophone criticism of her cinema to date on girls and girlhood discussed at the end of Chapter 1. Emma Wilson's discussion of the opacity of human subjectivity in 'Precarious Lives: On Girls in Mia Hansen-Løve and Others' (2012) brings out the opacity of the young girl subject in a way that emphasises it more than precariousness or vulnerability, the latter being the philosophical focus shared by Butler and Fineman (Fineman does not consider the representational aspects of subjectivity).

3   Corinne Renou-Nativel (2018) sees Gabriel's tendency to run away from almost everything as exaggerated and describes his relationship with Maya as 'a poignant story of failed love' (*une poignante histoire d'amour ratée*).

4   Sellier's suggestion here that virile, patriarchal masculinity was still in place in French cinema of the 1980s is controversial, given that critics such as Phil Powrie (1997) have dated a crisis in French cinematic masculinity to precisely this decade, but by mentioning just Delon and Belmondo as the stars illustrating such continuing domination, she is not necessarily making a general claim about that decade.

5   A rapid explanation of the 'autonomy orthodoxy' (what Fineman calls the 'autonomy myth') by contemporary continental philosopher Simon Critchley can be found in the first and second chapters of his *Infinitely Demanding: Ethics of Commitment, Politics of Resistance* (2012). Whereas autonomy is 'the basic principle of Kant's ethics' (p. 32), Levinas sees 'two main tendencies in Western philosophy: autonomy and heteronomy' (p. 56), and because autonomy has usually been dominant, 'sees his task as the attempt to breathe some life back into the latter' (p. 56).

3

Adversity and resilience: the post-secular ethic of vocation

Building on the exploration of Hansen-Løve's ethical vision of the precarious European family and of vulnerable subjectivity I have undertaken in Chapters 1 and 2, this chapter will extend analysis of some of her films in order to forge an account of the moral lives of their protagonists. These seem to be concerned mainly with struggles with adversity, and, in a second stage only partly reached by Victor (*All Is Forgiven*) and not reached at all by Grégoire (*Father of My Children*), with how they cultivate resilience through commitment to their work. As set out in Chapter 2, Camille of *Goodbye First Love* attempts suicide once Sullivan stops writing to her from South America, but draws on her interest in architecture – which she then pursues as a career – in order to recover from Sullivan's desertion. In *Eden*, when Paul's career as a DJ of garage music can no longer sustain him because musical tastes have changed, he (re)turns to literature, the subject of the dissertation he never finished in his early 20s. In *Things to Come*, Nathalie's remarkable (if sometimes emotional) resilience to life-changing events draws on the intellectual confidence she has acquired over many years as a philosophy teacher, and in *Maya*, the relationship Gabriel begins with Maya in Goa enables him to resume the working life he led as a war reporter before being taken hostage in Syria.

It is telling that five of these six films are fictionalisations of personal stories well known to Hansen-Løve: she drew on her own adolescence for the character of Camille; on her brother

Sven's DJ-ing career to write *Eden*; and on her parents' careers
as philosophy teachers for *Things to Come*. Even more important
than the personal sources of her material, however, is the type
of occupation pursued by her leading protagonists, which is
exclusively artistic or intellectual (or a combination of the two)
– architect, musician/DJ, philosophy teacher and war journalist.
In Hansen-Løve's world-view, it seems, artistic and intellectual
pursuits offer a kind of salvation – a source of reliable and enduring
meaning in a secularised Western world increasingly dominated
by capitalist economics and neoliberal values. In *Goodbye First
Love*, Camille explicitly describes her profession as 'a vocation', a
term 'born of a Christian context' and historically implying 'the
calling from God to fulfil a specific role by becoming a disciple
of Jesus' (Wheatley 2019: 316). We might well term this faith in
their work exhibited by the protagonists of Hansen-Løve's films
'post-secular' – a persistence of (or return to) religiosity and belief
amid constant economic and political uncertainty and crisis.
Post-secularity began to be a critical and theoretical topic in the
humanities during the so-called 'ethical turn' of the 1990s, then
came considerably more centre-stage in the 2000s, as the Western
world adjusted to terrorist attacks claimed by the Islamic organ-
isations of Al-Qaeda, ISIS and (more recently) Daesh – a forceful
entry of fundamentalist religion into world politics. To elucidate
the mix of the secular and the post-secular in Hansen-Løve's films,
which is evident well before the arguably more world-political
turn taken in *Maya*, this chapter will first introduce approaches
to the idea of the post-secular taken by the philosopher Jürgen
Habermas and the theorist-critic Manav Ratti. It will then engage
with the reading of Hansen-Løve's 'post-secular search for God'
offered by Catherine Wheatley, after which readings of *Goodbye
First Love*, *Eden*, *Things to Come* and *Maya* will be offered that
partly depart from Wheatley's interpretation of these films.

The English translation of Habermas's 'Secularism's Crisis
of Faith: Notes on Post-Secular Society' is prefaced by a short
introduction by Habermas himself, Tony Blair and Régis Debray
that announces 'the emergence of post-secular modernity'

(Habermas 2008: 16). The ironic idea of a crisis of faith in secularism arises, they propose, from '[t]he resurgence of political Islam and the endurance of religious belief in the most modern of societies – America' (2008: 16), and has been precipitated by the apparent failure of late twentieth-century secularism to 'generate any values beyond an indifferent tolerance of all belief' (2008: 16). As one of Europe's leading liberal intellectuals, Habermas's response to this crisis in values is to argue that secular citizens must be open to religious influence, and that Western secular societies should be positive towards and inclusive of religious minorities rather than rejecting and refusing to dialogue with them. Habermas finds the justification for this in the West's Judeo-Christian heritage, a source of morality and ethics and a key influence in shaping Western societies as they exist today. The emergence of post-secular modernity represents a major shift in the theorisation of modernity that has existed since the Enlightenment: it is not a rejection of Enlightenment rationality, but a recognition that modernity does not need to become ever more secular and atheist – indeed, that the assumption of a 'march towards secularism' (2008: 17) made by the secularisation theory may have been mistaken in the first place.

Habermas's argument in 'Notes on Post-Secular Society' concerns more than just the developed nations of Europe and the United States: he sets out how, in the twenty-first-century globalised world, 'orthodox, or at least conservative, groups within the established religious organizations and churches are on the advance everywhere' (Habermas 2008: 18), with Hinduism and Buddhism as well as the established monotheistic religions gaining ground across Africa and East and Southeast Asia.

> The transnational and multicultural Roman Catholic Church is adapting better to the globalizing trend than are the Protestant churches, which are nationally organized and the principal losers. Most dynamic of all are the decentralized networks of Islam (particularly in sub-Saharan Africa) and the Evangelicals (particularly in Latin America). (Habermas 2008: 18)

Against this background, the 'Occidental rationalism' that 'was once supposed to serve as a model for the rest of the world, is actually the exception rather than the norm – treading a deviant path. We and not they are pursuing a *sonderweg* ['special path']' (Habermas 2008: 18). Whether rising alternatives to secularism will in due course come to dominate Europe as well as Latin America and Sub-Saharan Africa is a question Habermas leaves open, saying that his impression is 'that the data collected globally still provides surprisingly robust support for the defenders of the secularization thesis' (2008: 19). He leaves no doubt, however, as to the vigour of religiously influenced regimes in the twenty-first-century world and the difficulties this poses for EU countries admitting large numbers of migrants and refugees from non-European states. After addressing the question of why secularised societies can now be termed 'post-secular' in the opening pages of his essay, he turns to the 'quite different, namely normative question':

> How should we see ourselves as members of a post-secular society and what must we reciprocally expect from one another in order to ensure that in firmly entrenched nation states, social relations remain civil despite the growth of a plurality of cultures and religious worldviews? (Habermas 2018: 21)

Since this question goes well beyond the ways in which post-secularity figures in Hansen-Løve's films, I turn at this point to the critic Manav Ratti, whose book *The Postsecular Imagination: Postcolonialism, Religion and Literature* treats the appearance of post-secularity in fictional narrative (in this instance literature) more directly than Habermas's philosophical and sociological approach.

In the introductory chapter, 'Situating Postsecularism', Ratti poses the following, challenging question: 'How can writers retain the best features of state secularism while also preserving the inspiring, generative, imaginative features of religious thought and practice, such as faith, awe, wonder, transcendence?'

(Ratti 2013: 7). Such 'inspiring' and 'imaginative' features have been widely observed by critics of Hansen-Løve's films, and I shall discuss these aesthetic tendencies, as distinct from the ethical implications of her post-secular approach to work as a vocation, in Chapter 4. The situating of post-secularism in cultural texts undertaken by Ratti is of relevance to the readings of Hansen-Løve's films I shall offer in this chapter through his discussion of 'enchantment' and of the distinction observed by Charles Taylor, another important thinker of post-secularism, between immanent and transcendent frames. Taylor has argued, particularly in *A Secular Age* (2007), that the pressure exerted by secularism on Western societies leads to the hegemony of the 'immanent frame' – 'the power of the observable material world to act as the regulator of what is real, true and knowable' (2013: 8). In religious societies, the prevailing world-view is regulated by a transcendent rather than by an immanent frame, allowing theistic beliefs and non-materialist ideas a role in shaping how those societies are run and governed. It is not difficult to see why literature, art and film are relevant to these debates: more than any other sociocultural area, they can encourage the maintenance of or return to transcendent rather than immanent frames, through their power both to express and to communicate wonder, awe, and other 'spiritual' states and feelings. Ratti focuses on 'enchantment' in the second section of the introduction to his book because of the longstanding association between secularism and *dis*enchantment, and asks whether faith, wonder and transcendence are not 'the irresistible dimensions of the human experience, infusing everyday life with richness, imagination and inspiration'? (2013: 17). If they are, literature and film clearly have a key role to play in relieving the oppressively immanent frames of neoliberal and heavily capitalistic contemporary Western societies.

Commentators such as Habermas and Ratti do not merely suggest that the secularisation theory of modernity may have been mistaken in the first place, and that it has given way to a post-secular modernity, they actively see this shift as a source of new forms of ethics for Western societies whose value systems have become exhausted. Ratti quotes political theorist William Connolly, who 'argues that modern secularism fails to provide for individual needs for ethics and reverence and hopes for a "non-theistic faith", one which can provide the need for enchantment, awe, and wonder, without the politicizing constraints of theistic and religious faith' (Ratti 2013: 20). It is with just such a non-theistic form of faith in mind that I now address its emergence in the way Hansen-Løve's central characters are bound to their professions, experiencing these as vocations or 'callings' that bestow meaning and value upon their lives.

In her article on Hansen-Løve and post-secular cinema (2019), Wheatley explores the search for immortality ('God') through artistic or intellectual work that is a feature of Hansen-Løve's protagonists' lives. Alighting on an exchange in an interview Hansen-Løve gave in 2016 about how to 'find meaning in life when we live in a secular world',[1] Wheatley recognises that 'her films are not "about" religion in any meaningful sense of the word', but states that 'religious imagery and theological allusions abound' in them (2019: 316), and that they also display 'a consistent thematic concern with vocation' (2019: 316). My more modest contention is that vocation as a sort of faith is the principal way in which the non- or post-secular features in Hansen-Løve's cinema, because it is in and through their occupations that her central characters do find meaning in their lives, and are protected from existential anxiety (the consequence of the death of God proclaimed by Nietzsche at the end of the nineteenth century). Although Wheatley fully seizes the importance of the protagonists' different types of work, and observes the aptness of the Christianised notion of 'vocation', she does not actually hold that Camille, Paul, Nathalie and Gabriel find enduring meaning or value in their work. They are, she states, '[u]nsure of what to believe in, ignorant of what they ought to do with their lives, [they are] lost, searching desperately for "the true good in order to follow it"' (2019: 322). '[C]asting around for a higher purpose – a way in which to imbue their lives with value or worth' (2019: 322), Hansen-Løve's central characters 'seek comfort in artistic work' (2019: 322) because the loss of God has left them so isolated and alone. Wheatley states that their occupational pursuits 'are markedly not mere displacement activities, nor are they simply jobs, means of getting by' (2019: 322), but still refers to these pursuits as '[the] seeking of solace' (2019: 322), which as will become evident in the following sections on *Goodbye First Love, Eden, Things to Come* and *Maya*, is not at all the language or attitude of the characters themselves. Wheatley's argument about the Christian connotations of vocation goes into religious history in a way I cannot fully retrace here, but she is at least ambivalent about the meaning and value that Hansen-Løve's central characters find in their vocations, saying that 'something like a feeling of disenchantment suffuses Hansen-Løve's careful renderings of the worlds of work her characters inhabit' (2019: 323), and that their jobs 'could so easily also be hobbies' (2019: 323). This does not correspond at all to my impression of the films: nothing is said in *Things to Come* to suggest that Nathalie Chazeaux is 'disappointed' (2019: 324) by her work, and to say that Paul Vallée is 'destroyed' by his DJ-ing career as Grégoire is by film production is definitely an exaggeration. The extent and force of the meaning and value afforded to Nathalie, Paul, Camille (*Goodbye First Love*) and Gabriel (*Maya*) by their vocations will become evident in the following readings of the four films in which an occupation proves as good as salvific.

Camille's architectural recovery

When Camille's parents and brother visit her in hospital after her suicide attempt, she is still just as tear-stained and inconsolable as when Sullivan left France, but on the table next to her bed is a copy of Le Corbusier's book *Le Modulor*, an exposition of the system of measurement the architect had developed over many years and published in the 1940s. Her brother asks if she doesn't have something more entertaining to read, to which she offers no reply. Camille's suicide attempt is dated to the spring of 2000 by a preceding scene at school, and when we next see her, her hair has been cropped in the manner she threatened Sullivan with in 1999. It is 13 September 2003, and she has evidently moved out of the family home to an independent flat in Paris, from which she is supplementing her student income with odd pieces of part-time work. On a visit she makes to the parental home, we learn that her mother is putting on a brave face about the departure of her father from their marriage.

Architecture becomes a central element of *Goodbye First Love* from this point onwards, as we watch Camille listen attentively to a tutor's critique of the model of a students' hall of residence she has designed and made. In a seminar that follows, a fellow student reads from Czech and Viennese architect Adolf Loos's essay *Ornement et crime*, first published in French in 1913 after being delivered in German as a lecture by Loos in 1910. Camille listens acutely to the following passage about how antithetical the home (*la maison*) is to the work of art:

> The home must please everybody, unlike the work of art, which does not need to please anybody. The work of art is the artist's private affair, which is not the case with the home. The work of art is not needed by the world, whereas the home fulfils a need [...] The human being loves everything that serves his comfort and hates everything that tries to prise him from his acquired and guaranteed position, everything that inconveniences him. This is why he loves home, and hates art.

This passage evidently chimes with Camille's thinking about how she wants to live – if not in a couple with Sullivan, then where and with whom? Her interest in Le Corbusier, like the student residence she has designed, reveals her to be thinking about collective forms of habitation, but her tutor has told her that the student rooms in her model are 'cupboards' (*placards*), way too small, and that the landscaping of the entire residence is imagined for solitary rather than collective living: rather than a hall of residence, what she has modelled is a monastery. Camille smiles

Figure 3.1 Camille drawing, *Goodbye First Love*

at this, obviously thinking of the solitariness of her life over the four years since the departure of Sullivan (Figure 3.1).

In the next scene, the connection between Camille's continuing mourning of her relationship with Sullivan and architecture is cemented, as she looks at a recent entry in her diary, which reads: 'Four years, and for what? Nothing, silence. Every day is just another day without him. *If only I had faith* (my emphasis). But I have a vocation. It's a reason for living. Isn't this tremendous (*immense*) in itself?' The emotional and spiritual equivalence Camille feels between love, religious belief and a vocational occupation is confirmed here. Belief in a God would have helped her forget Sullivan by putting the affair's importance in perspective, but since she has no faith, she has instead replaced it with an intense devotion to architecture, which she experiences as a 'calling'. It is hardly surprising that when she is asked why she wants to work in architecture by her tutor Lorenz, during a visit to the Kastrup Sea Bath near

Figure 3.2 Lorenz and Camille discuss architecture and careers, *Goodbye First Love*

Copenhagen (their first personal exchange), he is impressed by the mature commitment in her reply (Figure 3.2). Lorenz then volunteers that he took up architecture after failing to become a clarinettist, but that music would have been too solitary an occupation for him anyway: the implication that architecture is sociable because it is concerned with ways in which people may live together matches Camille's intuition, and the faith that she and Lorenz share in architecture's importance (as well as passionate interest in actual designs and projects) becomes central to the relationship that develops between them.

The words Camille writes in her diary about lacking religious faith are echoed by Hansen-Løve herself in the interview conducted for *The Film Stage* magazine in 2016 referred to above. When asked directly whether she is a believer, Hansen-Løve answers that although she is not, she wishes she were: 'even though, for me, there is no God, still the question of the quest for

God is very much present in all of what I'm doing.'[2] This applies to Hansen-Løve's leading protagonists as well as to the filmmaker herself, who would no doubt describe filmmaking as a vocation that is a reason for living. This way of thinking might be termed pre- or post-secular, but either way, it equates work with a quest for God rather than the 'proof of individual talent and industry' (Wheatley 2019: 322) it came to serve as in secular modernity. The quest for immortality through work is inherent in the activity itself rather than a result of having created works that will ensure one's name goes into the history books: architecture has become, quite simply, Camille's reason for living. And when her relationship with Sullivan resumes while she is living with Lorenz because of her inability to stop believing in the relationship, yet founders again due to Sullivan's unsuitedness to long-term partnership, Camille returns to Lorenz and to architecture and she visits the Ardèche and the scenes of her first love with Lorenz rather than with Sullivan, an indication that she has, finally, accepted a mature relationship in lieu of a youthful passion.

Paul Vallée's (re)turn to literature

At just over two hours, *Eden* is the longest film Hansen-Løve has made, and it follows Paul Vallée's life and work over more than twenty years, from November 1992 to December 2013. For over seventeen of these years Paul teams up with Stan de Man in the DJ-ing duo *Cheers* (written in the script of the eponymous American television comedy), until the particular kind of garage music in which *Cheers* specialises fades in popularity on the French music scene. Garage can no longer sustain Paul and Stan, although since Paul has had a cocaine habit and been increasingly in debt throughout his years in music, it is uncertain how lucrative the business has actually been. The popularity of garage with French and American club-goers has certainly sustained its own success over a decade and a half, allowing *Cheers* and fellow duo *Respect* to tour to New York and Chicago and invite singers from these cities to their club nights in Paris. Paul, Stan and the group of friends followed by the film pursue their passion exclusively: music's status as a vocation that fulfils them spiritually and emotionally is in no doubt, even if the word 'vocation' is not articulated explicitly as it is in *Goodbye First Love*.

As his DJ-ing career takes off, however, Paul is completing a thesis (*mémoire*) in creative writing, his likely literary talent having been noticed by an academic who has agreed to supervise him. Years later he has made little progress, and when he ignores a final reminder letter, the academic writes to tell him his registration on the degree is being terminated. Since this occurs before the peak of *Cheers*'s success, Paul is not especially concerned, but after the breakdown he suffers in his mid-30s, attending writing workshops becomes as immediate a priority as the telesales work he has to do to pay the rent. It is not Paul's interest in and passion for literature that was insufficient to allow him to become a writer, therefore, but the all-consuming character of the alternative 'creative' occupation of DJ-ing, whose advantages – the continuous company of like-minded musical people and renown within the niche world of house and garage music – are obvious. Economics, rather than lack of talent or a change in his artistic tastes (Paul still attends clubs and bars where he sees people from his former circle), is the main factor in his giving up DJ-ing, and even though a breakdown precipitates the career change, Paul is able to transfer his efforts from music and DJ-ing to literature and writing, the same shift made by Sven Hansen-Løve.[3] This is a substitution of one artistic occupation for another rather than a reneging on creative work in general.

As noted in Chapter 2, *Eden* follows not just Paul Vallée's years in garage music but the lives of some of his girlfriends and close male friends, at least two of whom are as creatively talented as Paul – aspiring graphic artist Cyril, already discussed, and his serious American girlfriend Julia (Greta Gerwig). Julia and Paul discuss her literary and his musical ambitions before she leaves Paris (where she has been waitressing) for her home city of New York, Paul trying to persuade her to stay in France by pointing out that a life in which she is a writer and he a DJ could work well. When *Cheers* tours to New York years later, Paul goes to visit Julia after a row with Louise, in the home she now shares with new partner Larry. Julia is heavily pregnant, but has also recently enjoyed the success of having a story published in the reputable literary magazine *Atlantic Monthly*. Like Paul, Julia and Cyril are artistically talented people not easily able to make a living from the field in which they practise.

A fragility in Paul is indicated in the first scene of *Eden*, when after taking ecstasy he spends part of the night outside, away from the rest of the group (an animated heron flying across the screen tells us he is hallucinating), so that Cyril has to come and find him in the morning. Paul turns out to be more socially robust than Cyril, perhaps on account of the stream of girlfriends (including three significant relationships) he attracts over his DJ-ing years. But the role Cyril plays in *Eden* is the important one of a kind of foil to Paul, who indicates the struggle creative work can entail, and the dangers of solitude and depression. Paul is not suicidally inclined like Cyril, and adjusts his life after his breakdown by giving up drugs and alcohol as well as by paying careful attention to money. In the final scene of *Eden*, alone in his flat, Paul erases the sketch of him Cyril drew on a domestic whiteboard years earlier, and replaces it with a shopping list. By giving writing a practical rather than an artistic purpose. Hansen-Løve seems to be reinforcing a major theme of *Eden*, the difficulties inherent in artistic occupations, and the danger of making oneself a martyr to them. Since the film then ends with a reading of a verse by American poet Robert Creeley about time and rhythm, it most certainly does not give up on the belief in artistic, creative occupations manifested across all Hansen-Løve's films to date.

Nathalie Chazeaux's philosophical resilience

In *Things to Come,* the vocation focused on by the film is scholarly and intellectual rather than artistic – teaching, and specifically the teaching of philosophy (the profession of both Hansen-Løve's parents). Nathalie Chazeaux, who exhibits extraordinary resilience in the face of several potentially devastating life-events, claims that a philosophical training is what sustains her through the transformation of her life brought about by the break-up of her marriage of twenty-five years and the decline and death of her mother. During the film, she also meets a lot of professional adversity caused by political and commercial change in the educational system and in publishing.

When husband Heinz breaks the news to Nathalie that he is leaving to live with another woman, she is shocked and disbelieving, but only for an instant. All we see of the break-up in process are scenes at the couple's Brittany holiday home that actually belongs to Heinz's family, then several in which Nathalie reacts indignantly to the sharing-out of the couple's enormous collection of philosophy books, seemingly with good reason, because Heinz takes the works of some highly significant authors, such as philosopher of ethics Emmanuel Levinas (Nathalie immediately re-purchases Levinas's *Difficult Freedom,* which she is seen opening on a train journey), and theological philosopher Martin Buber. In Brittany, Nathalie comments that she hopes Heinz's new partner likes gardening, because it would be a shame for the work and love she has put into cultivating the property's garden over many years to be wasted: Heinz immediately chides her for even mentioning the matter, to which Nathalie retorts that he rather than she is running away from the reality of their separation (Heinz has naïvely imagined that she will continue to visit the holiday home with their children, which she will not). An apparent lack of romanticism in Nathalie is demonstrated by the way she scoffs at a vase of flowers Heinz leaves for her in their apartment on the day he leaves, an incident Hansen-Løve deals with amusingly when the large bouquet will not fit in the kitchen bin and Nathalie has to take it out to the communal rubbish store: having disposed of the bouquet in the large IKEA bag she has put it in, she then returns to retrieve just the IKEA bag. Nathalie does not entirely lack romanticism, though: a second vase of flowers Heinz leaves for her later, rather than being instantly disposed of, is left on the coffee table in front of the sofa to contemplate, causing her to shed a tear.

Nathalie's toughness in the face of professional adversity is seen at the start of the film when she argues her way through a student picket outside her place of employment, the Lycée Paul Valéry. She tells students who have turned up to class that it is shocking that some of their number think they can control the actions of staff, then returns to the picket line to argue, successfully, for the admittance of four students who are not being allowed through. The strike, demonstrations and pickets seen in the film did in fact occur during Nicolas Sarkozy's term as president of France from 2007 to 2012, and by objecting to them Nathalie is not taking any kind of political position (she was a Communist party member in her youth but considers her politically active days to be over, we learn later): she was simply doing her job with the commitment and pride typical of her, evidence of a vocational attitude. On the one occasion in the film when she has to justify her actions in terms that could be considered moral or political (to Fabien, the former pupil whose anarchism she does not share or aspire to), Nathalie asserts that her aims have always been simply to teach young people (including Fabien) to think for themselves, further indication that for her, personal values are indissociable from professional activity (Figure 3.3).

A second way in which Nathalie is tested professionally in *Things to Come* is via her role as the editor of a series of philosophy textbooks with a prestigious Paris-based publishing house. When she calls in one day to collect copies of Fabien's book that he has requested (and that she finds she has to pay for), Nathalie is approached by two young marketing executives to be shown

Figure 3.3 Nathalie teaches philosophy outdoors, *Things to Come*

how the series' design is to be 'dumbed down'. Nathalie detests the new, jazzier design proposed to her, describing it with characteristic frankness as looking like an M&Ms advert. On a later visit she is told that the series is being discontinued altogether due to poor sales, but she accepts both decisions without a murmur of complaint, summing them up later to Fabien (whose second book was contracted for her series just in time) simply as 'I got sacked'. This incident shows an accurate awareness on Hansen-Løve's part of the marketisation of the academic publishing industry that has taken hold in the twenty-first century: the young publishing executives are charming, courteous and only very momentarily concerned by the effect of their decisions on Nathalie.

Where her depressed and demanding mother Yvette is concerned, Nathalie deals with the situation in an extraordinarily no-nonsense fashion, enviably balancing criticism with compassion. She visits Yvette at home when absolutely necessary (such as the day following a pleading early-hours phone call), and on one occasion leaves a class – an outdoor session in one of Paris's parks on how to approach the topic of truth philosophically – in response to her mother's repeated calls to her mobile, threatening suicide. When Yvette's calls upon the emergency services can no longer be controlled, Nathalie has her admitted to a high-class, expensive care home, confiding to her son Johann tearfully as they get in the car to go home that however comfortable the care home is, it smells of death. When Yvette is killed in a fall shortly afterwards, Nathalie arranges her funeral service in the Catholic parish church she rarely attended, with the causes of Yvette's psychological problems only emerging as Nathalie talks to the parish priest about her mother's life in preparation for the service – she suffered a 'thug' of a father and a mother who died young (meaning that Yvette was brought up by her grandmother), childhood illness, and three marriages which brought her little happiness. Having not had much of an education herself, Yvette insisted that Nathalie study and gain the qualifications that made her teaching career possible, a reminder of the link between vocation and family.

At the committal service for Yvette's coffin at a crematorium (rather than at the church service that precedes it), Nathalie movingly reads the famous passage from Pascal's *Pensées* known as 'Pascal's wager', in which the philosopher-theologian considers whether the human situation in the world makes religious faith a more advisable path than doubt ('I look on all sides and see only darkness . . . If I saw nothing there which revealed a Divinity, I would come to a negative conclusion; if I saw everywhere the signs of a Creator, I would remain peacefully in faith'). Wheatley suggests that this reading 'goes to the heart of the position in which not only Nathalie, but all Hansen-Løve's central characters find themselves' (Wheatley 2019: 322), and uses further words of Pascal's ('My heart inclines wholly to know where is the true good') in the title of her article. Although the position Nathalie allegedly shares with all Hansen-Løve's central characters is indeed, as Hansen-Løve herself puts it, one of 'existential loneliness',[4] it does not seem possible to state, on the basis of just this scene, either that Nathalie is endorsing Pascal's words or that all Hansen-Løve's central characters are in a situation parallel to that of Nathalie. Nathalie is certainly '[a]t her lowest ebb' (2019: 321), and probably wondering what source of strength will get her through the crises that have beset her life, but finds the answer to this question in philosophy and her vocation as a philosophy teacher, not in religious faith.

Two important consolations for Nathalie in her new life as a single woman are becoming a grandmother, and hosting Christmas dinner for her children and daughter Chloé's partner. At the hospital after the birth of Chloé's child - her and Heinz's first grandchild - over a year after the separation, Nathalie almost seizes the baby from Heinz, and then insists on holding him before her ex-husband (who has arrived first at the hospital) has been able to do so for as long as he would like. This is a comic rather than a serious moment, as Heinz and Chloé are both smiling broadly at Nathalie's impatience, and there is further comedy in Nathalie's insistence that baby Leonard resembles her, when everyone else agrees that he looks like Heinz, but it is less amusing when, after Heinz departs, she holds the baby for longer than her daughter can bear: Chloé dissolves into tears and Nathalie is slow to work out that this is because her own need to 'be grandmother' is getting in the way of her daughter's bonding process with her new baby. At the Christmas dinner not long afterwards, she more sensitively relieves Chloé of care for the crying Leonard in order to let her daughter relax and enjoy herself.

Predictably, the flat Nathalie used to share with Heinz becomes an emotionally and symbolically guarded space once Heinz no longer lives there: Nathalie is visibly relieved when (just before she welcomes her children in for the Christmas meal) Heinz finally returns his keys to her. Nathalie pointedly does not invite Heinz to stay, despite the fact that he has obviously carefully chosen this moment to retrieve a prized but mislaid book of philosophy, and in so doing, she effectively excludes him from any kind of communion with the family he left of his own accord. The meal Nathalie then cooks and hosts is full of quasi-religious sentiment, whereas Heinz will be spending the festival on his own, we have learnt, working, while his new partner spends it with her family in Spain. This final scene of the film overflows with very post-secular joys of feasting and family communion as Nathalie sings a lullaby to her grandson, a modestly magical conclusion to the film.

Gabriel Dahan, war reporter

Not a single scene of *Maya* shows Gabriel Dahan at work, since the film is made up of a kind of prologue showing the French state's reception of its newly released hostages, set for obvious reasons in Paris, and its much longer second section in India, where the action remains until almost the final scene. But these Paris- and India-based parts of the film are framed by two scenes in a hotel and an airport in Jordan (the gateway to the war raging in Syria in 2012 and 2013): in the opening one, Gabriel shaves off the beard that has grown during four months of captivity – an occasion for some contemplation in the bathroom mirror of the newly clean, re-Westernised image that results – while the film closes with a shot of the car speeding Gabriel and Frédéric away from the airport to the location of their next stint of reporting, a freeze frame classically suggesting openness to whatever the future brings.

In India, Gabriel hardly mentions his work to anyone: Maya only knows that he has recently been a Syrian hostage because her father Monty, Gabriel's godfather, has told her so. When she ventures to make Gabriel aware of her knowledge, he bristles and has nothing more to say about the matter, even if he does not actually reproach her for mentioning it. Excessively private about his working life when in holiday or family mode, Gabriel is also rather reticent when called to appear on camera in a professional capacity, such as at the official state welcome for the returned hostages, where he very obviously follows Frédéric at some distance down the plane's steps. In the prologue of *Maya* that sets up the main part of the film by explaining why Gabriel will be spending some months in India, he is perfectly at ease with everyone he mixes with, having no difficulty functioning socially as the war reporter that he is. He, however, betrays little of the intense commitment to his profession that is evident in conversation with the psychiatrist who specialises in the effects of captivity as a hostage, in conversations with Frédéric (in-person in Paris, by Skype while in India), and in his meeting with his mother in Mumbai, whose question about practising such a dangerous profession he answers by saying candidly that the high-risk job is there to be done and that he likes to feel useful. Perhaps most interestingly, but certainly most problematically from an ethical point of view, Gabriel's vocational commitment to war reporting is one of two reasons he gives to Maya for not continuing the relationship that begins towards the end of his time in Goa but is almost immediately suspended, before resuming two months later in ambivalent form.

The crux of the tension between Gabriel's interest in Maya and his defensive cleaving to his work as a reason for not having a relationship with her comes when they travel to Hampi and Agonda together, without Monty and Sigrid (as was planned). At the hotel in Hampi, Maya makes her romantic interest in Gabriel known when, after dozing on his shoulder as they watch television, he tells her to return to her own room to sleep and she responds by using what she previously told him are the only two French words she knows, 'Oh là là' and 'Dégueulasse!' (the second doubtless a knowing reference to Godard's *A bout de souffle* (1960), a French film Maya is likely to have seen). Gabriel plans to travel on alone to Agonda the following day but agrees to let Maya accompany him as long as her parents consent to this, which she untruthfully tells him they have. In the car that takes them to Agonda, Maya takes his hand, and when they go straight to the beach upon arriving, engages in some flirtatious swimming around and away from him offshore. At the end of the evening Gabriel finally takes her in his arms and kisses her, leading to some tender love-making, but it soon emerges the following morning that Maya did not ask Monty and Sigrid's permission to travel on from Hampi as she said she had, and that Monty is furious about this. When Gabriel reproaches her for lying to her parents, Maya defends herself by saying 'I want to be with you' and suggesting that she may be in love with him, to which Gabriel responds 'Listen! I don't want to be in love or in a couple or . . . anything similar'. He cannot stay in Goa long term: Maya would like to think she can accompany him to where his work is, because she is free, but Gabriel's riposte to this is that even if she is, 'I'm a war reporter, and it's my life'. The first part of this retort reveals Gabriel to be more conflicted about personal relationships than he admits to himself, but the second part, while spoken with some pride, is also defiant and defensive – a declaration of identity that decisively nips his new relationship with Maya in the bud. She makes it obvious to Gabriel as he packs her off home in a taxi and when they meet again months later that his behaviour has hurt her.

There is no reference in *Maya* to Gabriel seeing war reporting as a vocation, but his unexpressed commitment to his profession is glaringly obvious in the final scene of the film, when he slips some cash into the passport being checked by the Jordanian official and looks directly into his own eyes as his photo is taken. Here, easeful familiarity with procedures, his surroundings and himself replace the guarded defensiveness that has characterised his relationship with Maya. The lack of interest in and suitability for fatherhood I discussed in Hansen-Løve's male protagonists in Chapter 2 is all of a piece with Gabriel's use of his professional identity as a pretext for an involvement with Maya destined to be based on short, infrequent encounters: in a different manner to most of Hansen-Løve's earlier films, vocational commitment in *Maya* is firmly allied with a traditional masculinity exercised predominantly in the public, homosocial sphere. Commitment to a profession in Hansen-Løve's cinema seems unrelated to gender or any other kind of identity politics: it is, rather, ethical in a way that is linked to survival – being able to go on with one's life. Gabriel Dahan's being a war reporter may or may not be admirable, but it may be just as salvific for him as architecture proves to be for Camille in *Goodbye First Love* and DJ-ing and literature are for Paul Vallée of *Eden*.

Conclusion

Three of the leading characters discussed above pursue their careers in France (even if Paul's occupation as a DJ, in *Eden*, is inseparable from international musical trends). A strict separation of church and state has existed in France since 1905, and the wearing of the Islamic veil or any other sign of religious adherence in public is banned, a particularly rich site of secularism-related conflict in recent decades, with repeated rounds of protest when pupils have been dismissed from state schools for breaking the law by wearing headscarves or skullcaps. In the interview about *Things to Come* where Hansen-Løve is asked where Nathalie Chazeaux draws her 'inner force'[5] from, her answer links Nathalie's resilience to the meaning her vocation gives to her life, then suggests that finding meaning is harder in 'a secular world', and that secular France is therefore a particularly difficult place in which to do this ('It's not easy, especially in French society'.[6]) She implies, in other words, that the continuing strength of secularism (*laïcité*) in French society creates a hostile climate for the exploration of issues of belief and faith, and for the identification of meaning and value in individual lives. It is hard not to conclude that the non- or post-secular faith in vocation seen in Hansen-Løve's films discussed in this chapter arises out of the tense context of a still-vigorous secularist ideology that thwarts the very expression of all forms of religious sentiment. Despite not herself practising any established religion, Hansen-Løve's acute awareness of and experiential exposure to France's regulated expression of religious adherence makes itself felt in the devotion of her characters to their occupations, in which they believe with fervent intensity.

Notes

All translations, unless otherwise stated, are the author's own.

1   O'Connor (2016).
2   Ibid.
3   Writing under the name Sven Løve, Sven Hansen-Løve first published short stories in French and American reviews, followed by a collection of short stories in English in 2015, *Tender Neighbours*, then a novel in French, *Un emploi sur mesure* (Editions du Seuil 2018).
4   O'Connor (2016).
5   Ibid.
6   Ibid.

4

Candid camera, or an aesthetic of transcendence

In Chapter 3, we saw how Catherine Wheatley's work on Hansen-Løve's films has drawn attention to how their narratives engage with theological dimensions of human experience, through her protagonists' 'search for God' or a state resembling salvation. Hansen-Løve's vocabulary alone – forgiveness and the connotations of paradise in the titles of *All Is Forgiven* and *Eden* – confirms this tendency towards the theological as well as the philosophical, and both her use of certain locations and her manner of filming them (particularly in *Father of My Children*) produce unmistakeably Christian imagery. We might say that a certain spirituality, in the form of a clarity and power of emotion and intense romantic or family love, characterises all her films to date. This aspect of Hansen-Løve's filmmaking seems to arise both from personal inclination and from her cinematic influences, among whom she particularly counts Eric Rohmer and Robert Bresson (Catholic and Catholic-influenced directors respectively). She has stated that when she first viewed the films of Bresson, master of the so-called 'transcendental style', she identified immediately with the 'entirely bodily' mode of spirituality that animates Bresson's actors.[1] By articulating how religious belief contributed to shaping the film philosophies of Bresson and Rohmer and outlining Hansen-Løve's commentaries on their legacy and her consciousness of their influence, this chapter will explore the (Christian) theological dimension of her approach to filmmaking, and the type of images it produces. Focusing on the aesthetic rather

Figure 4.1 Basilica of Sant'Apollinare in Classe, Ravenna, *Father of My Children*

than the ethical dimension of the tendency towards religiosity identified in Chapter 3, this chapter will develop the account of Hansen-Løve's world-view begun in Chapters 1 to 3, analysing how her visual style combines the bodily and the spiritual in a manner reminiscent of both Christian theology and phenomenological philosophy. I shall begin with a discussion of Hansen-Løve's representations of children, physical passion and pastoral beauty, before moving on to the film philosophies of Rohmer and Bresson and their influence upon Hansen-Løve's image-making (Figure 4.1).

'Palpitations of life'

Early in a lengthy interview with Hansen-Løve for the radio channel France Culture, journalist Laure Adler explains that her personal appreciation of Hansen-Løve's first two feature films is that they overflow with the feelings of life (*sentiments de la vie*) or 'palpitations of life' (*palpitations de la vie*).[2] This leads in due course to discussion of Hansen-Løve's awakening to her desire for a career in cinema when she acted in Assayas's *Late August, Early September* in 1998, a shoot which, she says, convinced her that cinema is not just an 'art of life' (*art de vie*), but an 'art of living' (*art de vivre*), seemingly because it brings together the very different activities of writing and directing, which are solitary and demandingly sociable respectively. Hansen-Løve and Adler agree about the importance of 'life' to her films, therefore, but Adler's spectatorial view seems to point to an actual energy transmitted by them, the kind of energy seen in children's play and sexual re-lationships, as well as in the ethical emotions experienced when viewing art or scenes of natural beauty. Agreement with Adler's observation about Hansen-Løve's 'palpitations of life' leads me to start this chapter by dwelling on some of these particularly enlivening aspects of her films – the irrepressible playfulness of children in *All Is Forgiven* and *The Father of My Children*, physical passion in *Goodbye First Love*, and pastoral beauty in *All Is Forgiven*, *Goodbye First Love*, *Things to Come* and *Maya*.

All Is Forgiven begins with scenes of play, in which Victor is at home in Vienna and alone with Pamela on the morning of her sixth birthday. Encouragingly and gently he asks Pamela about the names of her dolls, and when his sister Martine telephones to wish Pamela a happy birthday, he gives her the phone to encourage autonomous action on her part. It is when father and daughter go outside to play with rackets and a ball, however, that actual playfulness takes over, as Victor both indulges his own greater adroitness with a racket and limits his dominance so that Pamela, who squeals and laughs as she runs around, has some chance to engage in the game. It is clear from these two brief scenes that despite the inability to hold down a job and stay sober that Victor will shortly demonstrate, he is both interested in and attentive to Pamela (albeit less constantly than her mother), and that Pamela is attached to him and unaware of anything 'wrong' with her father. Scenes of children's playfulness and play-acting also set up the domestic happiness of the Canvel family in *Father of My Children*, since when Grégoire eventually gets home to Sylvia and his children for the weekend after having had his driving licence confiscated for speeding, his younger daughters Valentine and Billie have prepared a version of French television's regular 8pm news programme. The rest of the family settles down on the sofa to watch the spoof, which is directed at Grégoire and earns his two younger daughters a spanking as affectionate as the spirit in which they prepared the miniature show.

The following morning, we watch Billie playing at building a model of some kind, so absorbed in the activity that she talks to herself, assessing her progress as she puts the puzzle's pieces together. Valentine, meanwhile, is still in bed and decides to hide under the covers, with the express intention of getting Grégoire to spot her ploy, which he does, announcing to the household that he cannot imagine where Valentine has disappeared to but then pouncing on her and indulging in a physical rough-and-tumble that makes her giggle and squeal. Hansen-Løve's observation of the interactions between children and parents in all these scenes is both acute and unusually oriented towards the children's experience: she renders childish excitement convincingly while also lending children's activity (such as Billie's model-building) interest and dignity, never trivialising the creativity that can be found in their play.

Given the centrality of Camille and Sullivan's relationship to *Goodbye First Love*, there are actually relatively few sex scenes in the film. Hansen-Løve elects instead to indicate the relationship's intensity indirectly, through its volatility and the way in which it influences the rest of the young protagonists' lives. Whereas Camille displays a seemingly hopeless romantic idealism, telling her mother that Sullivan is 'the one' [*l'homme de ma vie*], a preoccupation by the relationship that is causing her to cry all the time and sapping her of energy for other social relationships, Sullivan seems energised by Camille's beauty and her devotion to him, an energy memorably recorded in the film's opening sequence, where he cycles through the dawn to get condoms from a machine, also buying a red rose he tosses to Camille when he returns to her. It is this mismatch between the pair that causes the relationship to break down, since for Camille it is the most important thing in her life, whereas Sullivan is determined to travel to South America 'to become a real [that is, well-rounded] person'. However, it is the same discomfort with intense, committed relationships that causes Sullivan to leave Camille for the second time years later, and this now seems like an inadequacy on his part, while Camille's difficulty in definitively breaking up with Sullivan now seems more admirable – a genuine difficulty in moving beyond an unusual passion, rather than teenage idealism. This kind of even-handedness (or ambivalence) is one of the best indications of Hansen-Løve's skill at depicting profound and formative relationships: rather than taking sides with one character over another, which would bring in moral considerations, she sets out the stakes for both characters, and concentrates on the emotions involved, which if they are resolved (and typically they are not), only attain such resolution over long periods of time.

Pastoral beauty in France and India in *All Is Forgiven, Goodbye First Love, Things to Come* and *Maya*

The beauty of nature, particularly that of various regions of France, plays a regular part in Hansen-Løve's films, as early as her début feature *All Is Forgiven*, which is set mostly in Paris. In the closing scenes of the film the action moves to the Corrèze, in the Limousin region, which is the home of Pamela's step-grandfather, Paul. It is summer, and via the mediation of her aunt Martine, Pamela has just met up with her biological father Victor for the first time in over eleven years. Straight after these two meetings, for the second of which Pamela meets Victor alone (rather than with her schoolfriend Judith as on the first occasion), the scene cuts to children (Pamela's cousins, it emerges) playing in a river where they are catching tadpoles, and after Pamela joins them, the group walks back to Paul's home through rolling meadows and fields in glorious sunshine. With such a large and beautifully situated French country residence to spend her summers in, these scenes indicate how Pamela's mother Annette's second marriage to André has integrated her and their *famille recomposée* into the bourgeoisie in a way that her first marriage to Victor could never have done: Victor's inability to hold down a job meant that it was only in her native Vienna (where the family lived for several years) that Annette could live comfortably. But first and foremost, the beauty of the Corrèze seems to intervene in *All Is Forgiven* to indicate the pleasure and joy that might result from the re-acquaintance of Victor with his daughter, on both their parts: Victor writes to Pamela while she is away in order to say how much it means to him that they have been reunited (all too briefly as it turns out), and Pamela replies almost instantly. The phone call that brings the news of Victor's death abruptly punctures the timeless beauty of Paul's Corrèze home, after which Victor's funeral takes place in Paris, but the film then returns to the Corrèze, and in an apparently symbolic final scene, Pamela asks to be excused from the family table, where nothing related to Victor's life or death can be discussed because of her mother's inability to do so, and walks away into the greenery surrounding the house. It is only in Nature and not in bourgeois comfort, it seems, that Pamela can find some solace for her biological father's unexpected early death.

It is in *Goodbye First Love* that the pastoral beauty of France plays the largest part in Hansen-Løve's work to date. During their initial relationship early in the film, Camille and Sullivan take a holiday at her parents' second home in the Ardèche, which has wonderful views onto the surrounding countryside of valleys and mountains, sited as it is on a grassy slope with orchards around and below it. Sullivan climbs a tree from which he can speak to Camille as she opens shutters in the bedroom they choose to sleep in, and the couple then go out into the countryside: Sullivan befriends and mounts a horse and helps Camille climb up behind him for a short ride, and while out walking they stumble across a picturesque unoccupied dwelling that Camille says is her 'dream house' (*maison de mes rêves*). The couple then pick and eat cherries growing wild, just as Jean Renoir's characters did in *Partie de campagne/A Day in the Country* (1936). This sequence ends with a carefully framed image of the couple embracing in a sunny clearing that seals the link Hansen-Løve is making between natural beauty and their physical love, and although Camille and Sullivan then fall out due to the different expectations they have of relationships, pastoral scenes reoccur when they have made up again, with the fifteen-minute 'Ardèche' chapter of the film closing on scenes of the couple hiking to and swimming in the Loire river, happily and playfully enjoying one another's company again (Figure 4.2).

In the traditional literary sense, pastoral is a genre found from the classical to the Romantic eras, depicting a bucolic society far

Figure 4.2 Sullivan and Camille swim in the Loire, *Goodbye First Love*

from the complexity and corruption of the city, and although the natural beauty of French regions such as the Limousin and the Ardèche in Hansen-Løve's films may not be pastoral in this sense, it seems to function in the same way for her characters. In *Things to Come* Nathalie twice visits her former pupil Fabien at the farmhouse retreat he has bought with his German friends and girlfriend Elsa in the Vercors, where they live cheaply in order to be able to write and publish. The second visit has the purpose of making the household a gift of her mother's obese black cat Pandora, in a symbolic completion of Nathalie's mourning for her mother (Pandora has been Nathalie's domestic companion since her mother went into care, and shocks Nathalie on her first Vercors visit by 'reverting' to a life of hunting birds and vermin she has actually never known). This brief second visit takes place in winter, but the first one occurs in summer heat, when the mountains, meadows and scenery of the Vercors are at their most beautiful: as Nathalie arrives and discovers the farmhouse's idyllic location, she exclaims: 'It's paradise here!' One scene in particular during her visit illustrates the importance of the region's natural beauty, when we see Nathalie walk through a wood alone (it seems to be early in the day) and emerge onto a grassy hillside with a magnificent vista of snow-capped mountains beyond, where she looks around in wonder before choosing a comfortable spot to lie and read in the sun (Figure 4.3). On another occasion everyone living and staying at the farmhouse decamps to a nearby river and waterfall where they swim and sunbathe, Nathalie on her own and Fabien with Elsa, but the sense of the restorative power of Nature is just as strong as that of Nathalie's solitude. In the Vercors episodes of *Things to Come*, just as in the closing scenes of *All Is Forgiven* and parts of *Goodbye First Love*, Hansen-Løve's protagonists experience Nature in much the same way as in the tradition of pastoral literature: despite the entirely different historical context of a very earth- and ecology-conscious twenty-first-century Europe, natural beauty calms and refreshes them, as well as instilling wonder, functions that are ethical as well as aesthetic.

Figure 4.3 Nathalie in the Vercors, *Things to Come*

A rather different spin is put upon the natural beauty of the Goan landscape in *Maya*, insofar as tourism is Goa's main industry (many of the beaches seen in the film are crowded and lined with bars, cafés and nightclubs). When Gabriel awakes from the one-night stand with a tourist he spots dancing alone in a club shortly after first meeting Maya, the dominating view of the palm-lined beach and an inland lake he gets from the balcony of her rustically styled accommodation is breathtaking – a Goan version of the idyllic beach views sought by tourists worldwide (Figure 4.4). Away from the coast, lush tropical vegetation and abundant wildlife is everywhere: Maya and Gabriel explore a ruined fortress overgrown by greenery, spotting an eagle overhead, after returning from the boat trip with Monty, Sigrid and their friends where they have seen dolphins swimming nearby, and observe exotic parrots near the Hazara Rama temple a few days later. The ample garden of Gabriel's inherited villa-style house has run completely wild and needs as much attention as the house, and the much more cultivated gardens of the Nilaya

Figure 4.4 Gabriel glimpses a typical Goan beach, *Maya*

hotel, situated in what used to be jungle (as Monty tells Gabriel when first introducing it to him), serve as the backdrop to several important conversations between Gabriel and Maya. Despite the crowds of tourists and tropical location, the beach-oriented lifestyle of swimming and sunbathing Gabriel avails himself of while in Goa serves a similar purpose to the more traditional kind of pastoral leisure offered by France's Corrèze, Ardèche and Vercors in Hansen-Løve's earlier films – relaxation, refreshment and reinvigoration.

A transcendental style for the twenty-first century? Hansen-Løve's aesthetic of transcendence

In an interview conducted after the release of *Father of My Children* in 2009, Hansen-Løve answers the question of what the French New Wave means for her by evoking the cinema of François Truffaut and Eric Rohmer in particular. She likes 'everything' of Truffaut's, she says, while with Rohmer, whose work strikes her as cerebral and 'wordy' (*du côté de la parole*) – a quality widely observed of Rohmer's films – 'what stays with you after having seen them is the physical feeling of a mystery, of something invisible. With him, extreme clarity opens onto the deepest mystery' (Frodon 2009: 28). This is very theological vocabulary, which befits the inclination of some of Rohmer's work towards questions of faith and doubt: his first really successful film, *My Night with Maud/Ma nuit chez Maud* (1969), has been viewed as a dramatisation of Pascal's wager, in which the seventeenth-century philosopher proposed that men might bet with their lives on whether God exists or not. Rohmer was a devout Catholic who kept his personal, family life and his film-making work separate, and did not often treat theological or religious issues (*My Night with Maud*, one of the 'Six Moral Tales' Rohmer made between 1962 and 1972, being an exception), but he did sometimes speak or write about the links he saw between cinema and Christianity. Hansen-Løve does not comment on these, but has evidently been influenced by more than just the 'mystery' in Rohmer's films, since in the same interview she indicates that it was in part through sympathy with the wordiness of the films of Rohmer and Truffaut (and also Jacques Doillon) that she developed a cinematic style distinct from the 'mute cinema' (*cinéma mutique*) finding favour with many of her young contemporaries (Frodon 2009: 28). In such work, the capacity of speech to convey truth – the 'pho-nocentrism' deconstructed in favour of an emphasis on writing and difference in the work of Jacques Derrida (1930–2004) – is neither respected nor exploited. The popularity of almost wordless films among various filmmakers of the decades between the *Nouvelle Vague* and the 2000s made it seem '[a]s if speech were superficial and that truth lay only with bodies. I don't believe this, and don't want to be classified as making this mute kind of film, which my early shorts reacted against by containing many dialogues' (Frodon 2009: 28).[3] In their employment of speech and dialogue, Hansen-Løve's features to date resemble Rohmer's as much as they do those of many of her contemporaries,[4] allowing us to think that she would like the mystery and invisibility not opposed to the clarity of language that she observes in Rohmer's films to be detectable in her own – a question I shall return to later in this chapter.

Another pre-New Wave French director who has evidently influenced Hansen-Løve is Robert Bresson, whose film-making career began before and during the Second World War but did not really take off until after it, with *Diary of a Country Priest/ Journal d'un curé de campagne* (1951), *A Man Escaped/Un condamné à mort s'est échappé* (1956) and *Pickpocket* (1959). Faith and religious belief figure frequently in these films, with *Diary of a Country Priest* adapting the novel of the same name by French Catholic writer Georges Bernanos and telling of an idealistic young parish priest's suffering and failure to integrate into the community. The experience of redemption has always been recognised as one of Bresson's most important concerns in his story of the eponymous thief of *Pickpocket*. In 1966, the American critic Susan Sontag devoted a chapter of her book *Against Interpretation* to Bresson, entitled 'Spiritual style in the films of Robert Bresson', in which she offers the view that Bresson's 1950s films are 'spiritual' not on account of their content but on account of their spare, undecorative, anti-dramatic form. Belonging to a poorly understood tradition she calls 'the reflective or contemplative' (Sontag 1966/2009: 179), these films are often found to be cold and remote, which is, Sontag explains, why the critical success of Bresson's cinema always outstripped its popularity with the viewing public. In Sontag's view, however, this detachment is an effect of a particular way it has of mediating its emotional power. In '[g]reat reflective art', she maintains, '[t]he pull toward emotional involvement is counterbalanced by elements in the work that promote distance, disinterestedness, impartiality. Emotional involvement is always, to a greater or lesser degree, postponed' (Sontag 2009: 177). The critic and filmmaker Paul Schrader was to extend this view of Bresson's style in *Transcendental Style in Film: Ozu, Bresson, Dreyer*, where he expounds a thesis that these and 'other directors in various countries have forged a remarkably common film form' (Schrader 1972: 3). Rather than being 'determined by the film-makers' personalities, culture, politics, economics, or morality', this form is the result of 'the desire to express the Transcendent in art and the nature of the film medium' (1972: 3). I am not suggesting here that Hansen-Løve's style directly imitates Bresson's, since it is not at all spare, distanced, disinterested or remote, and it is unclear how her contemporary stories of families, children and adolescents would accommodate such a style, but Bresson is a director she esteems, and who exerted a particular influence on *Father of My Children*. This influence was transmitted via Humbert Balsan, the producer on whom the character of Grégoire Canvel is based, who played the role of Gawain in Bresson's 1974 film *Lancelot of the Lake/Lancelot du lac*, and was second assistant director to Bresson on *The Devil Probably/Le diable probablement* (1977). With this connection of Balsan with Bresson in mind, I shall set out next how *Father of My Children* might, despite its contemporaneity, be termed 'Bressonian'.

In an interview with *Cineaste* magazine conducted amid the initial screenings of *Father of My Children* in the US in March 2010, it is suggested to Hansen-Løve that Bresson's spirit hovers over the film, even if his name is never mentioned. She replies that the lack of specific references to Bresson 'is deliberate since, as a director, I want to create my own language and my own references' (Porton 2010: 11), but continues:

> But there's the question of the influence Bresson had on Humbert Balsan. When I went for the first time to visit Balsan in his office on Rue Montmartre, I remember that there was a very large *Lancelot du Lac* poster on the wall behind him. And he was also very proud to show me the view from his window of L'église Saint-Eustache, where one of the most important scenes in *The Devil Probably* was shot. (Porton 2010: 11)

As a meditation on suicide (its main protagonist Charles eventually commits suicide in circumstances also interpretable as murder), *The Devil Probably* would seem to have been an important film for Balsan, but despite the latter's legendary status in the French film community as the pro-auteurist producer of directors like Claire Denis, Elia Suleiman and Béla Tarr, the community was at a loss to explain or understand his suicide in 2005, the year after Hansen-Løve's visit to him to discuss his interest in producing *All Is Forgiven*. Hansen-Løve's explanation of Balsan's career trajectory is that '[h]e would have liked a career as an actor. When he realised that this wasn't possible, he found another way of nurturing his love for film that was perhaps even better than being an actor' (Porton 2010: 11). She and Balsan 'had a bond in that we both started as actors' (2010: 11), and she describes her encounter with him as 'probably one of the two or three most important I've had in the world of cinema' (2010: 11). This closeness does suggest that her interpretation of Balsan's character and of Bresson's influence upon it may be accurate. Just as with the importance of Catholicism to Bresson, Balsan had had a Jesuit education, and an intimate knowledge of the history of Christianity is an element of the character of Grégoire Canvel emphasised in *Father of My Children*.

Several scenes in *Father of My Children* illustrate this knowledgability on Grégoire's part, which is never commented on by his professional colleagues, perhaps because they are ignorant of it. Within walking distance of the family's country home in the Loire valley is a ruined chapel built by the Knights Templar that they visit on the very weekend Grégoire has had to hand his driving licence over to the police. Announcing that this is not just any chapel, Grégoire explains the history of the Crusades to the Holy Land and the history and identity of the Knights Templar to his younger daughters, who are more interested in climbing a ladder abandoned inside the ruin (which Grégoire forbids) than in his history lesson. This is a short scene whose emotional resonance only becomes fully apparent after Grégoire's death, when Sylvia and her daughters revisit the chapel to sit in silence and remember him. A brief shot of the abandoned ladder, pointing heavenward, recalls Grégoire's authority in Christian matters, both intellectually and as the *pater familias*, even if his suicide can be considered to mark him a failure at fatherhood. Sylvia and the three girls return home in silence, a tight-knit group of mourners illuminated by the setting sun.

In another scene during the family holiday to Italy cut short by Grégoire's breaking of his promise to Sylvia not to conduct business on his mobile while away, Grégoire's familiarity with Christian art is demonstrated as he explains the meaning of a basilica's mosaic-studded dome to Valentine and Billie: Saint Apollinaire, the first Christian bishop, is surrounded by a number of sheep symbolising Christ's disciples (the sheep on its own is Peter, while John and James are the two sheep huddled together). Despite his daughters' greater interest in running around the church trying out a spy-glass or lighting a candle, Grégoire succeeds momentarily here, as he did in the Knights Templar chapel, in getting his audience to listen to his lesson and even to make observations about the dome's mosaics. Hansen-Løve's camera picks out the details of these as they are mentioned, and the climax of the scene is a brief shot of the disembodied hand of God at the top of the dome, which Grégoire indicates to Valentine and Billie by imitating the hand's gesture of pointing (although in the reverse direction). A proximity and even an identity between Grégoire and God is obviously being suggested by this shot, one which takes on meaning through Grégoire/Balsan's thorough familiarity with and influence by Christian history and art.

Another scene in Ravenna in *Father of My Children* offers Hansen-Løve a further opportunity for religious symbolism: the family are bathing in a stream and some rockpools whose waters are chalky white rather than clear. Valentine swims wearing only the bottom half of a bikini, so that her flat, pre-pubescent chest is visible as well as the sun-imprinted silhouette of her bikini top (images that might conceivably have been objected to in 2010 if Hansen-Løve had not already proven herself an excellent and respectful filmer of children). As she immerses herself fully in the milky white water, Valentine throws back her head and paddles around on her back with only her head protruding, so that her head is framed by the water and her face illuminated by shafts of sunlight – the very image of a baptism or other religious rite, in which Valentine's youth and vulnerability are emphasised and the opaque water means that only her head and face can be seen.[5] Mixing Christian imagery with the pantheistically inclined appreciation of Nature observed as 'pastoral' earlier in this chapter, this is a powerful and unforgettable scene despite its brevity, where Hansen-Løve's *mise en scène* and cinematography are far more important than the inconsequential narrative action.

Scenes such as the ones in Ravenna described above, like the bleaker images of addiction and breakdown seen in *All Is Forgiven* and *Eden*, confirm the considerable emotional power of Hansen-Løve's dramas. This power functions in a remarkably calm and balanced fashion: there is never so much as a hint of melodrama (in which the spectator is absorbed by and buffeted around by characters' dilemmas), and nor is the spectator detached and distanced from emotional drama as with Bresson's 'spiritual style' as explained by Sontag. The importance Hansen-Løve attaches to speech is certainly part of the reason for this calm and balance, since the films' dialogues offer sufficient articulation of characters' states of mind to make them intellectually engaging as well as emotionally profound. But the depths of feeling Hansen-Løve plumbs are far from fully explored and explained – in other words, her narratives do unquestionably hold some of the invisibility and 'mystery' that Hansen-Løve finds in Rohmer's cinema. There are several possible ways of accounting for this, of which the first is her rejection of authorial omniscience, and another is what she herself calls 'ambivalence':

> There's an ambivalence that you find in all my films, perhaps because it's part of my personality. But it might also have to do with the fact that I never went to film school. I've been very lucky to be able to write films as a

kind of translation of my world view, without having to
pass through a screenwriting system, full of ideas about
what's good and bad, efficient and inefficient. I've always
had confidence in the spectator: in their ability to put
together a story, to manage ellipses, to fill gaps. I think
it can be stimulating for them. And that's why my films
are perceived as so ambiguous. At film school they teach
writers to say things very clearly, it's more black and
white – I'm simplifying, of course – but in effect I have
the right to write in shades of grey because no one ever
forced me to be more explicit. (Wheatley 2016: 27)

One example of this ambivalence might be the relationship
between Nathalie and Fabien in *Things to Come*: is Nathalie
attracted to her former pupil as is suggested by her family's
reaction when Fabien calls briefly at their apartment early in
the film, when Chloe and Johann are visiting their parents? If
she is – and her relationship with Fabien certainly becomes one
of intimate friendship when she confides in him about the end
of her marriage – then this is never actually *visible* or explicitly
acknowledged by Nathalie.

Ambivalence and a rejection of authorial omniscience are
two factors contributing to the sense of 'mystery' retained in
Hansen-Løve's cinema, but another equally important one, I
propose, is the very understanding of human (inter)subjectivity
with which she works, indications of which are provided both
by her academic background and the film-critical vocabulary she
uses. Hansen-Løve is not just the daughter of two philosophy
teachers, since she herself completed a Masters' thesis on the
German phenomenological philosopher Max Scheler, the author
of a 1913 treatise entitled *On Sympathy*. An allusion to the philosophical idea of sympathy occurs at the start of *Things to Come*,
during the visit to Chateaubriand's seaside grave that Nathalie
and Heinz make in Brittany: it is windy, and Nathalie is inside
the boat's cabin marking essays while Heinz and their children
are out on deck, as the camera tracks slowly in to show us the
title of the piece of work she is reading – 'Can one put oneself

in the place of the Other?' And in an interview about *Father of My Children*, Hansen-Løve agrees that there may be parallels between her interest in phenomenology and her chosen career: 'Looking back on it, I see that there are some parallels that I'm drawing on. The book [*On Sympathy*] deals with universal sympathy, empathy, alterity, concern for others. And these are all issues that are dealt with in cinema' (Jones 2010: 56). Hansen-Løve's familiarity with Schelerian phenomenology, I suggest, does not just contribute to the measured, contemplative style of her films, but indicates an adherence to the anti-Cartesian understanding of human subjectivity shared by most phenomenologists (Husserl, Scheler, Heidegger, Merleau-Ponty). In this understanding, consciousness is embodied and material, rather than the seat of a rational mind separated from a purely mechanical body. Phenomenology undoes the mind-body dualism established by Descartes in the seventeenth century and develops a 'monist' rather than a dualist understanding of human subjectivity, according to which the mind works with and through the body rather than separately from it. The influence of phenomenological monism on Hansen-Løve can help to explain the mixed approach she takes to the body in film, whereby bodily action is essential to how she works with the medium (it constantly conveys her characters' desires and motivations), but in which she is suspicious of allowing bodies to be the sole site of truth, insisting that this belongs just as much to language. Her acquaintance with phenomenological philosophy can also explain the use she often makes of the term 'incarnation' to describe the power of embodied speech in the cinema – the films of Rohmer being her usual example.[6] In addition to its theological sense of the materialisation of the Holy Spirit in the person of Christ, 'incarnation' is used by Christian phenomenologists such as Gabriel Marcel and Scheler (Scheler was the son of a Lutheran pastor and an Orthodox Jewish mother who converted to Catholicism in the 1910s) to refer to the incarnation of language – one sense of *logos* – in the flesh. This sense of incarnation is still a theological meaning, but describes the consubstantiality of word and flesh (*logos* and *corpus*) rather than the incarnation of God in human form.

Finally, and perhaps most importantly, Hansen-Løve's interest in the philosophical idea of sympathy can help to explain how spectatorial alignment with her film characters is never exclusive, but is shared: in *All Is Forgiven*, it is shared between Victor and Pamela; in *Father of My Children*, between Grégoire, Sylvia and Clémence; while Sullivan in *Goodbye First Love* and Maya of *Maya* share 'protagonist' status with the leading characters Camille and Gabriel respectively. As a director, Hansen-Løve might be said to exhibit an ethical generosity towards her characters, always sympathising with more than one of them and never taking sides in their disputes. Her understanding of and feeling for her characters is profound, but is combined with a great deal of ambivalence as seen in their unexplained actions and reactions. As viewers, we feel deeply *with* and sometimes for the characters, but are not encouraged to sympathise with one rather than another, and are not offered any metalanguage with which to pick over characters' emotional states. To view a Hansen-Løve film is to enter into the screen world her characters inhabit and experience it with them, phenomenologically.

Candid camera

A striking quality of Hansen-Løve's filmmaking is the lucidity with which it represents a huge range of human emotions, from joy and intense romantic love via depression to desperation. Her focus on feelings is penetrating without being analytic: emotional states such as Camille's despair at Sullivan's inconstancy are un-flinchingly visually conveyed, and feelings are frankly expressed verbally by those characters inclined to such expression – most of the films' main protagonists, though it applies less to Nathalie Chazeaux and Gabriel Dahan in the films from 2016 and 2018 than to most of the characters in the earlier films. One way to describe Hansen-Løve's treatment of the profound currents of feeling that characterise her cinema is 'candid', which has connotations of artlessness and ingenuousness as well as directness and frankness, and has been used of her work by commentators such as Emma Wilson, whose description of Grégoire Canvel's lesson to his daughters about the mosaic-covered dome in Ravenna runs as follows: 'Yet the film is so understated, there is such simplicity, naturalness and *candour* in the editing and in the rhythm of the conversation, that the symbolism does not disrupt the sure, smooth realist surface' [my emphasis] (Wilson 2012: 280–1). Candour is also a word Hansen-Løve herself uses regularly, for example of the 'mixture of candour and deeply moving intelligence' (Frodon 2009: 28) found in François Truffaut's films, which she ascribes to the closeness to childhood Truffaut maintained throughout his life.[7] Other synonyms for 'candid' in addition to 'frank', 'honest' and 'outspoken' are 'free from malice' and 'informal', adjectives which fit Hansen-Løve's characters' emotional dispositions and the tenor of her narratives well: she concentrates on the everyday and is entirely unconcerned by 'special' or ceremonial events or occasions. With these observations in mind, candour is a quality of Hansen-Løve's filmmaking I shall dwell on a little further to conclude this chapter.

One obvious connection to candour in Hansen-Løve's work is the ready use she makes of the word 'truth' when talking about it, which derives, it seems, from having had a philosophy-teacher father not unlike the character of Heinz in *Things to Come*, a Kantian who lived his life according to the categorical imperative.[8] By 'truth', Hansen-Løve certainly does not mean the visual accuracy of her representations (truth in the sense of the Latin *adequatio*), but something more akin to the authenticity held in high esteem by existentialist thinkers, in opposition to the inauthentic 'bad faith' into which it is easy to fall. She depicts her characters in a manner that may be described as 'truthful', in that they appear as rounded, complex and frequently conflicted human beings. Examples of candid behaviour and expression in the films are Camille's insistence to her mother, in *Goodbye First Love*, that love is the only thing that matters to her, and Nathalie's frank voicing of disgust when she is shown new cover designs for her book series in *Things to Come*. And honesty prevails: there is hardly an instance of mendacity or deception across all the films, unless Camille's concealment from Lorenz of her resumed affair with Sullivan is held to be deceitful.

Etymologically, the adjective 'candid' derives from the Latin *candidus*, from the verb *candere* meaning 'to be white' or 'to glisten'. The word therefore alludes to the many qualities of the colour white, some of which are purely aesthetic – brightness and shining visibility – and some of which are moral, such as simplicity and honesty. The name of Voltaire's Candide, surely the most famous literary figure associated with candour, alludes to the inflexible simplicity with which Candide over-persistently believes in the optimism of his tutor Pangloss (the Leibnizian optimism that is the target of Voltaire's satire). While the phenomenological being-with her characters to which Hansen-Løve invites the viewer works against any authorial position-taking on the outcome of the films' narratives, it is probably fair to say – as I suggested throughout Chapter 3 by focusing on 'adversity' and 'resilience' – that they combine great difficulty and pain for the protagonists with consistently sanguine conclusions, which could be likened to the narrative of *Candide* (1759). An association can also be seen between 'glistening' white candour as a designator of race or ethnicity and Hansen-Løve's film-world, the socio-political whiteness of which was remarked upon by early reviewers, especially those writing about *Father of My Children*. While such criticisms of a blinkered ethnic whiteness are arguably fair in relation to the way this film foregrounds Christianity via the character of Grégoire Canvel and in its imagery, *Maya*'s main location of India and figuring of Maya herself and her father Monty as important non-white-skinned characters, along with Gabriel's close colleague Frédéric as a black Frenchman, could be seen as a riposte to those inclined to criticise conservativeness of racial representation in Hansen-Løve's films.

In this chapter I have traced the abundant 'feelings of life' in Hansen-Løve's cinema, evident in her depictions of play and playfulness, romantic love, and pastoral beauty, and explored the relationship her cinema has with the films and thinking of Rohmer, Bresson and the so-called 'transcendental style' associated with Bresson and other major directors in the 1960s and 1970s. I have suggested that her film-making style has affinities with phenomenological philosophy that may have been influenced by her philosophical background and education, and that this non-omnisicient, ambiguous or 'ambivalent' style reinforces the combination of profound emotion and non-partisan perspective found – that is, findable by the viewer – in her film narratives. Since the style leaves much to uncertainty and the unknown, or 'mystery' if we use Hansen-Løve's theological vocabulary, it participates in the aesthetic of transcendence set up in scenes of pastoral beauty and intense love. Many of the characteristics of Hansen-Løve's style – directness, frankness, ingenuousness – can be termed 'candid', and to describe her filmmaking in this way captures a complex value very suggestive in a twenty-first-century woman filmmaker.

Notes

All translations, unless otherwise stated, are the author's own.

1   'Hors Champs', interview with Laure Adler broadcast on France Culture, 20/5/2010.

2   Ibid.

3   Hansen-Løve both acknowledges and limits the resemblance of her use of dialogue to Rohmer's by saying 'The way in which language progresses is the music of Rohmer's movies. In my movies, I believe that the internal music rests on a type of equilibrium between talking and silence. This means that there is a lot less dialogue in my films than in Rohmer's. There are scenes with long dialogues but there are also a lot of long moments which are purely impressionist, like landscapes' (Ganjavie 2016: 9–10).

4   Fiona Handyside has given extended consideration to the connections between Hansen-Løve and Rohmer on speech and dialogue, in 'Words for a Conversation: Speech, Doubt and Faith in the Films of Eric Rohmer and Mia Hansen-Løve' (Handyside 2019). As she eloquently observes, 'Rohmer was renowned for his use of direct sound, working with

sound engineers such as Jean-Pierre Ruh and Claudine Nougaret; he favoured placing his characters in natural amphitheatres or in sealed-off environments (park benches surrounded by foliage, dips and hollows, cars, courtyards), so that their speech could be recorded as clearly and cleanly as possible without the need for overdubs or post-production work. Hansen-Løve, too, uses this technique. The effect is at once eminently theatrical and entirely ordinary, as the world itself becomes a stage, and voices are contextualised by their sonic environments (wind, birds, traffic, crickets, music). The visual style of the films also works toward helping the viewer to focus on the significance of dialogue. Camera work tends to eschew close-ups in favour of longer shots that show us bodies interacting with their environments, so that gesture and position are important to the performance and how dialogue is to be interpreted. Words are spoken in a carefully delineated real world, articulated by individuated characters whose physical, corporeal presence gives the words heft, grain and tone. Speech is embedded into a world rendered to us through the devices of cinema – colour, movement, sound, texture, light' (Handyside 2019: 11–12).

5   This is the second of the two scenes given extended commentary by Emma Wilson in the 'Precarious Lives' article discussed in Chapter 1. Rather than religious symbolism, what Wilson is drawing out of the scene is its implications for Valentine's identity as a girl: 'her disappearance into the milky liquid [seems] almost a figure for the intermittence of identity, for its rhythmic, serial qualities. Hansen-Løve finds an elemental, liquid setting for a scene that interrupts her narrative, and immerses the viewer suddenly and unexpectedly in the sensory field of a girl protagonist' (Wilson 2012: 281). Valentine's constant motion and the privileging of embodied experience and the senses over 'sense' gives an Irigarayan or Merleau-Pontyan twist to this excellent commentary, although the critic whose influence Wilson acknowledges is Martine Beugnet.

6   Hansen-Løve comments in interview that 'the fact that the great thing about cinema is this idea of "incarnation" and the employment of real bodies for fictional purposes' [. . .] 'must have been one of the topics I discussed with Humbert [Balsan]', and adds 'This idea has traumatized me – in a good way' (Porton 2010: 11). Handyside's article on dialogue in Hansen-Løve's and Rohmer's films (Handyside 2019) makes only passing mention of the embodied character of speech in either director's films, when embodiment is clearly fundamental at least to Hansen-Løve, who comments that 'any dichotomy between words and actions is a false one. "I like filming characters talking" [. . .] "The voice, the body, their position – this is physical too"' (Wheatley 2016: 25).

7   It should perhaps be noted that the French *candeur* and English *candour* do not seem to translate one another exactly, dictionaries suggesting that *candour* should be rendered by the French *franchise* or *sincérité* (both words that seem to have more exact English equivalents in 'frankness' and 'sincerity'), and that *candeur* corresponds to 'ingenuousness' rather than 'candour'.

8   Hansen-Løve refers to her father's 'Kantian rigour' and her mother's 'Rousseauistic tendency' in an interview with Mathilde Blottière about *Goodbye First Love* (Blottière 2011).

5

Lost in music

According to Miguel Mera and David Burnand, 'writing that examines the common themes, practices, methodologies and ideologies of music within European film tradition is scarce' (2006: 1), which is because 'the vast majority of extant research has concentrated on a canon of Hollywood film music' (2006: 1). The quantity of studies of music in European film(s) has increased since Mera and Burnand wrote these words in 2006, but in his recent study *Music in Contemporary French Cinema: The Crystal-Song* (2017), Phil Powrie echoes their observation, noting that at the time of writing his book, 'there are only three monographs in English specifically on music in the French cinema, all of which focus on earlier periods' (Powrie 2017: 4), and that 'French-language studies have in their turn focused mainly on Hollywood' (2017: 5). Partly for this reason, Powrie draws on 300 French films made between 2010 and 2015 as a corpus on which to ground the second half of his book, which he intends to focus on twenty-first-century French cinema (despite including films made from the mid-1980s onwards, because heritage cinema, which took off in France, as elsewhere, in the mid-1980s, is an area to which he devotes particular attention). Since commentary on music in twentieth- and twenty-first-century French film is only to be found in article form on particular directors, composers and films and as chapters in geographically wider-ranging books, I shall offer a brief summary of the historical trends in the use of music in French cinema itself and how this has been approached by critics, as a basis for the exploration of Hansen-Løve's film music that follows.

In Mervyn Cooke's history of film music (2008), Britain and France are the only European nations to get a whole chapter to themselves, but Cooke offers an especially useful account of the importance of individual composers (Maurice Jaubert, Joseph Kosma, Georges Auric and others) to classical French cinema up to the post-Second World War period. After suggesting that the New Wave 'arguably did more to revolutionize the techniques and aesthetic perspectives of film music – and all other parameters of film production – than any other movement in the history of cinema' (2008: 319), Cooke switches to a director-based approach in which he details the continuing importance of composers such as Michel Legrand to Godard, and Georges Delerue (whose score for Godard's *Le Mépris/Contempt* (1963) may be his best known) to Truffaut, from *Tirez sur le pianiste/Shoot the Pianist* (1961) onwards. As period settings became more important to Truffaut after 1970, he adopted the interesting practice of re-using Jaubert's 1930s scores (for example in *L'Histoire d'Adèle H./The Story of Adele H.* (1975)) as part of a strategy of disinhibiting his actors: 'carried by the music, [actors] will not be afraid of stylized gestures which they would reject if asked to do them cold' (Truffaut in Lacombe and Porcile 1995, quoted in Cooke 2008: 328). Other New Wave directors turned to contemporary classical and sometimes avant-garde composers – Alain Resnais to Hans Werner Henze and Krzysztof Penderecki and Claude Chabrol to Pierre Jansen - but as Cooke observes, '[m]odernism in French film music suffered a setback when leading composers such as Duhamel and Jensen defected – the former to work in musical theatre in the 1970s and the latter to television in the early 1980s' (2008: 332). Michel Legrand was successfully lured by Hollywood, where he won Academy Awards for his scores for *The Thomas Crown Affair* (dir. Norman Jewison, 1968), *Summer of '42* (dir. Robert Mulligan, 1970) and *Yentl* (dir. Barbra Streisand, 1983), and by 1980 Georges Delerue had gone to Hollywood as well (Cooke 2008: 333). Maurice Jarre, who had found fame there earlier with his Oscar-winning music to David Lean's *Lawrence of Arabia* (1962) and *Doctor Zhivago* (1965), espoused what Cooke describes as 'a refreshing reversal of traditional European views', remaining 'heavily critical of what he saw as intellectually arrogant and professionally sloppy attitudes in French cinema that he felt were no comparison to the discipline and devotion to duty of the Hollywood artisans' (2008: 334). Jarre did particularly inventive work with European director Volker Schlöndorff (especially *Die Blechtrommel/The Tin Drum* (1979)) as well as in the US. It may therefore be a mistake to see the moves to the US of composers like Legrand and Delerue as a loss to French cinema, and more constructive to interpret the practice of composers working both in Hollywood and in Europe as anticipating the contemporary age of post-national film industries in which musicians of all nationalities regularly work beyond their country of origin as well as in it. As Kathryn Kalinak points out at the start of her introductory study *Film Music* (2010), it is only recently that critical writing on film music has expanded to take the sort of global perspective that she considers now to be necessary, a perspective that moves beyond its undisputed origins in the United States and Europe to ask questions about Japanese, Indian, Iranian and Brazilian cinema (2010: xiv).

A vital choice facing any contemporary director except those whose films barely feature music at all, such as Austrian Michael Haneke, is whether to work with a composer in order to provide their film with an original score, or to rely on existing music and songs to do this. As Kalinak sets out in the first chapter of *Film Music*, we can still speak about a 'musical score' in the case of films that have had no original music composed for them, but this approach (familiar to anyone who has bought a CD of or downloaded the music used in a particular film because they like the selection) is known as a 'compilation score' (Kalinak 2010: 5). When a musical selection is 'culled from a variety of pre-existing sources' (2010: 5) in this way, a music supervisor may be employed who 'works to realize the vision of the director'

(2010: 5), but in the case of auteur cinema such as Hansen-Løve's, it is more likely that the director themselves will choose the selection: Kalinak cites Quentin Tarantino, Wong Kar-wai and Pedro Almodóvar as typical instances (2010: 5). It is also still common for auteur directors to work with composers: in contemporary French cinema, the now internationally renowned French-Greek composer Alexandre Desplat has scored the majority of Jacques Audiard's films, while the more France-based Philippe Rombi has worked regularly with François Ozon as well as scoring blockbuster comedy *Bienvenue chez les Ch'tis/ Welcome to the Sticks* (dir. Dany Boon, 2008) and two films in the *Asterix* franchise. In interviews, Hansen-Løve has spoken more than once about her dislike of composed rather than compilation scores, saying that:

> [I]t's not something that appeals to me. This is because it's often the case that a film is made and a score is written and the music is meant to push the film along and that's its sole purpose for being. Whereas I think that the musical choices I make are not meant to comment on the action but to open other doors so the audience can think about what's happening in different ways. (Porton 2010: 14)

In other words, Hansen-Løve dislikes the way music tends to be used in composed scores, solely in relation to the film's narrative: in my view, her films do occasionally employ music as a 'narrational force' (the second sense of the deliberately ambiguous expression 'Narrative Film Music' in the title of Claudia Gorbman's acclaimed study *Unheard Melodies: Narrative Film Music* (1987)[1]), but in them, no music has been written for the express purpose of 'push[ing] the film along'. I shall return to general questions about Hansen-Løve's compilation scores such as the effect of the score on the film's narrative, the language(s) used in its songs, and how the score is likely to work on the audience's emotions, after an introduction to the types of music she includes and some analysis of each of those types.

Music in Hansen-Løve's films

Eden, which is the only one of Hansen-Løve's films to date to be co-written (with her brother, French ex-DJ Sven Hansen-Løve), is partly devoted to charting the rise and fall of garage music, defined as 'house music plus disco', between the early 1990s and 2011. Many of its sequences feature parties and raves at which international stars of house (Frankie Knuckles, Terry Hunter) perform, and 'Lost in Music', the second, shorter half of the film, depicts how the film's DJ protagonists give years of their lives to their 'art', to the exclusion of the material concerns that preoccupy most contemporary twenty- and thirty-somethings. As well as serving as a tribute to the early life and career of Sven Hansen-Løve, then, *Eden* documents an entire musical movement, yet the film's music credits are barely more extensive than those of *All Is Forgiven* and *Goodbye First Love*, in which music – particularly folk, but also classical and pop – plays a hugely important role. Musical tracks in these and the four other films offer commentaries on narrative situations, on protagonists' states of mind, and, in three particularly memorable instances in *Goodbye First Love* and *Things to Come*, on the passing of time. In Hansen-Løve's films, music does fulfil its traditional function in film, which is to convey mood and atmosphere, but it also articulates characters' feelings, structures and gives dynamic to wordless narrative sequences, and supplements the articulation of important themes such as parental love and the loss of romantic love. Hansen-Løve's soundtracks are composed of contrasted parts of dialogue, silence (with accompanying background noise) and music, and bear distinctive rhythms assembled from the roughly equal use of these three major components of film sound. The following account of how Hansen-Løve employs music in her films is structured into the categories of classical, folk and pop music respectively, and I will mention but not dwell on the other elements of her characteristically rich soundtracks. I shall then provide a full analysis of the generically distinctive *Eden* not offered in earlier chapters, before concluding the chapter with the reflections on general questions about her compilation scores promised above.

1. Schubert, melancholy and lyricism

The music of Franz Schubert, a composer central to the Romantic movement, figures prominently and memorably in both *Things to Come* and *Maya*, where a serenade is sung diegetically by Judith Chemla in her role as Gabriel's ex-partner Naomi. Piano music by Schubert's younger German contemporary Robert Schumann as well as part of a Beethoven piano sonata are also heard live in *All Is Forgiven*, when a cousin of Annette's called Nektar (Elena Fischer-Dieskau, granddaughter of the famous baritone Dietrich Fischer-Dieskau and a successful professional pianist) plays two pieces from Schumann's 1848 'Album pour la jeunesse' at a family party in Vienna. A sympathy and even an attraction between Nektar and Victor seems to be hinted at when she gives him a volume of poems by the Austrian Expressionist Georg Trakl that Annette insists on reading from aloud, presumably to thwart further acquaintance-making between her husband and Nektar. Victor's evident pleasure at the gift nonetheless prefigures the affair he will later have with Gisèle, to whom he is first attracted when he sees her dancing to music.

The Schubert *Lied* that cuts in to the action of *Things to Come* as Nathalie is urgently called away from Heinz's Brittany holiday home for the final time, to see her mother in Paris, is a song called 'Auf dem Wasser zu singen' performed by Dietrich Fischer-Dieskau and Gerald Moore, a famous duo in Schubert song cycles. The music's extra-diegetic status does not even slightly lessen the efficacy with which the scurrying piano accompaniment conveys the swift and deep currents of emotion Nathalie is feeling at this point, and of which we are reminded when the song reoccurs over the film's closing credits, directly after its sentimental final scene. The performance of a Schubert song by Naomi early in *Maya*, which she is persuaded to give at the café reception where family members and friends welcome released hostages Frédéric and Gabriel home, is of a serenade unnamed in the film's credits, but its words are unlikely to be of importance anyway. There is both great beauty and immense sadness in the melody that fills the silent café, whose lights have been dimmed at Naomi's request, in order to make the performance less intimidating for her rather than to enhance its effect on her audience. There is irony as well as melancholy in the fact that her song is a serenade, of course, since although Gabriel may savour its emotional effect upon him, it has no influence at all upon his wish not to resume the relationship with Naomi that ended before he went to Syria. (Frédéric may be thinking this might happen when he suggests Naomi sing, after reporting that he knows the effect her voice has on Gabriel, but if so, the suggestion is in vain.) Two versions of this Schubert serenade occur in *Maya*, the second being an evidently very well-known arrangement for guitar by the nineteenth-century Austro-Hungarian guitarist Johann Kaspar Mertz, which we first hear over the otherwise silent sequence showing Gabriel's solo trip across India not long after he arrives. It lends a reflective and melancholy mood to his journey that serves to prepare for the tense meeting with his mother at the end of the trip: since Gabriel never subsequently comments to anyone on whether the trip lived up to expectations it is hard to know what his experience of it was, but it certainly seems to confirm and deepen his connection to India rather than the opposite. Like the Schubert song in *Things to Come*, the serenade reoccurs over the film's closing credits, indicating its structural importance to *Maya*'s mood and action.

2. Feelings of Celtic folk

The use of Scottish singer-songwriter Matt McGinn's 'Corrie Doon' (1968) in *All Is Forgiven* immediately drew attention to the acquaintance with Celtic folk music that Hansen-Løve turns to advantage in her first three films. The Gallic expression

'Corrie Doon' may loosely be translated as 'cuddle down', identifying the song as a lullaby like English singer-songwriter Duncan Browne's 'Berceuse' ['Lullaby'] that is heard over the final credits of *Father of My Children*, after Doris Day's recording of 'Que Sera Sera'. 'Corrie Doon' plays over the dialogue-free scene of Pamela and her friend Judith taking the metro home from Pamela's first meeting with Victor for over eleven years, expressing the tenderness of Victor's love for his daughter more fully than any words could do, even if the silence, lighting and cinematography of the scene are also essential to its emotional power. In *Goodbye First Love*, Matt McGinn's 'Little Ticks of Time' (1969) strikes up extra-diegetically as Sullivan buys the hat for Camille that she will wear on two holidays in the Ardèche some years apart, and continues as the couple travel there and explore Camille's parents' house together. 'Little Ticks of Time' is quick, restless and performed in a staccato style by McGinn, in contrast to the expansive and lyrical contemporary folk song Hansen-Løve selects to accompany the final scene of *Goodbye First Love*, English musician Johnny Flynn's 'The Water' (2010), performed with Laura Marling. Here Camille returns to the same stretch of the river Loire where she and Sullivan swam years earlier, wearing the hat Sullivan bought for her, temporarily alone:[2] forgetting to weigh down the hat with stones as she does her other clothes, Camille watches as a strong gust of wind picks it up and carries it downstream. As the lyrics of 'The Water' describe the healing properties of water's capacity to bear aloft, and lift out of an oppressive, destructive situation, it is of course tempting to apply them to the transition to a 'mature' relationship that Camille has finally made (marked by the loss of the hat), even if she did not particularly aim to do so. But the difference in rhythm and mood between Patrick Street's 'Music for a Found Harmonium', which accompanies the first river swim, and 'The Water' is equally if not more expressive of how Camille's life has changed in the eight or so years since her holiday with Sullivan, testament to the range of styles and emotions to be found in folk music.

It is in *All Is Forgiven* and *Goodbye First Love* that we find the greatest number of folk songs in Hansen-Løve's films. The former features Scottish songsters Rory and Alex McEwan's 'A lum hat wantin a croon' (1957) and 'Marie Hamilton' (1956), and the Black Country Three's 'Three Ravens' (1966)). In *Goodbye First Love* we hear the Irish folk tune 'Paddy Ryan's Dream/Mama's Pet' (1969) performed by Seamus Tansey and Reg Hall, and Andrew Cronshaw's arrangement of the traditional 'Wasps in the Woodpile'. This may invite suggestions that the two films have a similar compilation score. Also in *Goodbye First Love*, however, are two songs by the Chilean songwriter, composer and visual artist Violeta Parra, 'Volver a los 17' (1966), which accompanies a moping Camille to school and at home one Friday when she does not expect to see Sullivan that weekend, and the well-known 'Gracias a la vida' (1966), which plays suggestively over several scenes as Camille and Sullivan's relationship resumes eight years after he broke it off. The song is playing in the Latin quarter bar where the couple meet and seems to be diegetic, but this proves otherwise as it continues over their evening walk back to the flat Camille shares with Lorenz, and resumes as Sullivan walks home alone. Along with these two films and *Father of My Children*, where what sounds like a version of the traditional English 'Greensleeves' performed on acoustic guitar by folk-rock singer-songwriter Cliff Aungier – in the credits the track, composed by W.C. Aungier, has the title 'Blue Sleeves' (1969/2000) – is found alongside Duncan Browne's 'Berceuse', *Things to Come* also makes meaningful use of non-Celtic folk music. Here, Nathalie and Fabien listen to American Woody Guthrie's 'My Daddy Flies a Ship in the Sky' as Fabien drives Nathalie between the station and his farm-cum-commune, and, charmed by the lyrics, she remarks how different the type of music is from the unvarying diet of Schumann and Brahms her husband Heinz listened to during their married life, a comment that seems almost to refer to the generation gap between her and Fabien. Another Anglophone folk voice listened to by Fabien is that of Scottish-born Donovan, whose haunting 'Deep Peace' is playing at night during Nathalie's second, brief visit to the farm when she comes downstairs to talk because she cannot sleep. The song seems to indicate the contentment and fulfilment Fabien is finding in his rural-yet-intellectual life in the Vercors: folk music is associated with Fabien as a person in a way it is with no other character across Hansen-Løve's films. Another traditional French song that could be called a folk song – the lullaby 'A la claire fontaine' – is important in bringing *Things to Come* to its conclusion. Nathalie sings it to her baby grandson at the Christmas Eve dinner for her children, and, because Isabelle Huppert performs the song herself, it fittingly seals her pre-eminence in the film as character and star.

3. Pop-mobility: from the family home to the rave parties of *Eden*

Where classical and folk music are concerned, the identity of the performer(s) and recording is of importance to the effect a piece or song will have when used in a film scene, but these are arguably even more important when it comes to pop music, where 'covers' of tracks by different artists tend to express their personal interpretations more strongly. Hansen-Løve chooses a less well-known recording of a familiar pop song on at least two occasions, the first being 'Lola', where it is the 1979 recording by The Raincoats playing at the party in *All Is Forgiven* where Victor gets to know Gisèle, rather than The Kinks' better and enormously well-known original. The second is when 'Unchained Melody' plays at the end of *Things to Come*, where it is a 1959 recording by The Fleetwoods that we hear and not The Platters' 1956 or Roy Orbison's 1969 version, let alone The Righteous Brothers' 1965 recording famously employed in *Ghost*, the Patrick Swayze and Demi Moore vehicle from 1990. In *All Is Forgiven*, 'Lola' plays diegetically along with several other The Raincoats tracks as Victor watches Gisèle dance and is attracted to her, whereas the intense love described by the lyrics of 'Unchained Melody' is evidently familial love in this instance, because the location is Nathalie's flat, where she is entertaining her two children and new grandson to dinner. As the song plays, the camera executes an unusual reverse move out of the bedroom where Nathalie has just sung a lullaby to her grandson, Huppert's unaccompanied voice giving way to the rich harmonies of The Fleetwoods' a cappella singing, then backs further down the flat's hallway towards the front door. It comes to a stop in a position where Nathalie and her grandson can be seen, but in the sitting room that has come into view, we see the Christmas tree and decorations rather than her children, reinforcing the scene's emphasis on religiously inclined festivity. Perhaps the only other occasion in Hansen-Løve's films where music conveys love as strongly and memorably as 'Unchained Melody' does here is the motorbike ride Gabriel and Maya take at the end of the film, when he has to beg her to leave the party going on at the Nilaya hotel in order to join him in private because she has not forgiven him for his behaviour two months earlier. The playing of Nick Cave & The Bad Seeds' 'Distant Sky' (2016) as they ride leaves the unexpressed intensity of Maya and Gabriel's feelings for one another unambiguous, while also linking those feelings to the Goan landscape through which they are riding – since the song's lyrics speak of setting out for 'distant skies'.

The only scenes where dance music is heard in Hansen-Løve's films apart from its many occurrences in *Eden* are a brief passage of *All Is Forgiven* where Pamela and her friend Judith arrive at a night club where Lionel Catalan and Sven Hansen-Løve's 2006 track 'People' is playing, followed by the same composers' remix of Sebastien Teller's 'La Ritournelle'; the couple of occasions in *Maya* where Gabriel visits open-air dance venues in Goa; and the sequence in *Goodbye First Love* following the three-year ellipsis after Camille's suicide attempt. Here she dons a blonde wig, spangly blue top and red skirt to work as an usherette at an unidentified event where the tracks 'Frank Sinatra 2001' by Miss Kittin & The Hacker and 'Now That Love Is Gone' remixed by Fata Monteco play diegetically.[3] If there is always a diegetic link between Hansen-Løve's use of dance music and filmic action, however, this certainly does not apply to pop music in general, particularly in *Father of My Children*, to which it is probably more important than any other film except *Eden*. Just as Doris Day's extremely well-known 1956 recording of 'Que Sera Sera' plays over the final credits to reinforce the open future faced by Sylvia, Clémence, Valentine and Billie, Lee Hazlewood's 'The Girls in Paris' (1967) places the film's female characters in their metropolitan environment with an unmistakeably 1960s sound and style. (Hazlewood is the composer of 'These Boots are Made for Walkin', first recorded by Nancy Sinatra at the end of 1965 though covered by dozens of other artists since).[4] The pop-rock mixture and country sound of these Doris Day and Lee Hazlewood songs also characterises all *Father of My Children*'s other musical tracks except the folk songs 'Blue Sleeves' and the lullaby 'Berceuse' already referred to: John Leyton's hit 'Johnny Remember Me' (1961) has a galloping rhythm and blue notes exactly like Jonathan Richman & The Modern Lovers' tracks 'Egyptian Reggae' (1977) and 'South American Folk Song' (1977) heard over the film's opening sequence, as Grégoire walks through streets of Paris to his car while continuing to conduct business on his mobile.[5] The combination of energy and melancholy conveyed by the rhythmic beat and harmonic blue-ness of 'Johnny Remember Me' and both Jonathan Richman & The Modern Lovers tracks exactly expresses Grégoire's personality, and Hansen-Løve's choice of similarly bold, rhythmic and tuneful but female-oriented 1950s and 1960s tracks for the later part of the film indicates considerable skill in modulating the tone of her filmic material.

In her review of *Eden* for *Film Comment* (Jones 2015), Kristin Jones calls the film an 'intimate chronicle of the development of the French electronic music scene' (2015: 67). 'Chronicle' may not qualify formally as a film genre,[6] but seems an entirely apt moniker for the ambitious temporal scope – twenty-one years – over which *Eden* charts the music played by DJ-ing teams *Cheers* and (to a much lesser extent) *Respect*. The ultimate financial failure of Paul Vallée/Sven Hansen-Løve does not seem to have been shared by his *Cheers* partner Stan de Man (real identity

Greg Gauthier), and certainly did not happen to the French electro duo best known internationally, Daft Punk, whose music figures several times in *Eden* and whose enormous success and popularity is openly compared to the limited careers of Paul and Stan. (A running joke in *Eden* sees Thomas and Guy-Man – the abbreviated names of Thomas Bangalter and Guy-Manuel de Homem-Christo, by which they identify themselves – regularly go unrecognised at club entrances until one of their peers involved in organising the party identifies them as 'les Daft Punk', upon which they are immediately admitted.) The film is also extremely ambitious in its staging of tens of rave parties attended by hundreds of people, many of which were filmed in New York at a 'secret' club SRB Brooklyn (Blondeau 2014) (Figure 5.1): the budget required by so doing and Hansen-Løve's failure to secure *avance sur recettes* funding meant that several producers reneged on the project, finding it too expensive and too long. Hansen-Løve cut four hours to just over two and abandoned

Figure 5.1 *Cheers's* outdoor party in NYC, *Eden*

her original plan to shoot entirely non-digitally before Charles Gillibert took it on and saw it through, for a budget of just over €4m (Lalanne 2014b). Securing permissions to (re-)use the music of many internationally known artists was a long and complicated process, despite being assisted by Sven's contacts (2014b), and in an interview given to *Libération*, Hansen-Løve claims that she spent two years working on how to make the sound of the club scenes authentically 'incarnate' (Gester & Péron 2014).

Eden's achievement in documenting the movement of garage music in France, located primarily in Parisian clubs le Rex, the Queen and le Djoon (Gandillot 2014),[7] is perhaps all the more impressive given that her brother's career is an extremely personal story for Hansen-Løve, who idolised her elder brother (eight years her senior) when they were growing up. In a particularly full article and interview she gave to *Les Inrockuptibles* (Lalanne 2014b), Hansen-Løve explains that she started work on the film just as the bankruptcy of Sven's *Cheers* label forced him to quit music as a profession, and Sven confirms that co-writing the film with his sister 'was a way of finally turning the page and devoting myself to literature, which was what I really wanted' (2014b). Hansen-Løve had been the person to whom Sven played his first mix-tapes in the early 1990s, when she was just ten, and he had resumed relations with the parental home after a period of rupture he enforced by leaving home aged sixteen. She regularly attended the parties he began to run at Paris's What's Up bar from 1995 onwards, loving what she describes as the lyricism of garage music more than its electronic pulse (2014b) Despite never taking drugs or drinking much at raves, Hansen-Løve was, like her brother, addicted to the sense of communion around which they revolved, and shared his nocturnal lifestyle to a considerable extent throughout her student years, until she began writing for *Cahiers du cinéma* in her early twenties. (Sven was, unsurprisingly, also a cinephile.) She explains very precisely to *Les Inrockuptibles* that she did not formulate *Eden* simply as a project to help her brother out at a difficult time, cinema being the living that was by then sustaining her, personally and financially, but states that:

> I did nonetheless think that writing this film with me could allow him to rethink his past and find a meaning in it that might have escaped him. Even if, of course, I mainly made the film to help myself – so that it could bring me out of a dangerous depression by recounting something broader and more collective than my previous films. (Lalanne 2014b)

Sven had no inclination to tell his own life story, despite feeling capable of writing fiction (which he went on to do), but maintains that he could not have written the film on his own (Lalanne 2014b)

A very particular mood is being sought by Hansen-Løve in Eden's club night scenes, summarised by Paul Vallée in an interview he and Stan give to Radio FG (a station on which they already have their own weekly show) early in *Cheers*'s success: the piece of music they choose to represent their tastes is MK & Alana Simon's 'The MKappella', whose sound Paul describes as 'both delicate and rousing (*entraînant*), quite hypnotic [...] somewhere between euphoria and melancholy'. These words echo those Paul speaks to a DJ after the very first party night of the film, in a submarine somewhere far out of the city, when in trying to identify a track he heard the night before, Paul describes it as '*sort of* happy [my emphasis], with quite a gentle melody . . . tiny flutes . . . small sounds'. Once the DJ has found the LP and put it on, this music drowns out the conversation of the party-goers by continuing extra-diegetically as they walk through woods in early daylight, beginning the trek home. Although the mass of people dancing at raves, as well as the DJs themselves, appear ecstatic and euphoric, the electronic pulse of the music and the robotised voices used by musicians such as Daft Punk match an artificiality in their (often cocaine-fuelled) communal pleasure. The crowd frequently sings along with the songs' lyrics - 'Follow Me' by Frankie Knuckles, 'Promised Land' by Joe Smooth, 'Lost in Love' sung by Arnold Jarvis who visits a *Cheers* night from the

US. As the group of friends (minus Cyril) settles into the accommodation found for them on their New York visit, Daft Punk's 'One More Time' strikes up and is played in its entirety as we see an accelerated compilation of shots of gigs in Chicago and other cities that form part of the tour. Another entire song interpolated in this section of the film is Terry Hunter's 'Time and Time Again', a perfect example of the blissful communion fans find at the rave, whose final words are 'And now I know paradise'. Stars of the house and garage music scene who appear in the film are Arnold Jarvis, Terry Hunter (who plays Paul his new song 'Your Love' when Paul visits him in New York) and Crystal Waters, who sings 'Gypsy Woman' live when she comes to Paris: love, time and music itself are recurrent themes of the euphoric, reality-oblivious songs in which dancers and DJs alike lose themselves, with the regularity of the club night scenes in the film working on the viewer in the same way that the music draws its proponents in and will not let them go (Figure 5.2). The melancholy that accompanies the euphoria of this music is inseparable from rhythm – not only of

Figure 5.2 A typical Paris rave party, *Eden*

the music, but of the addictive pleasure it affords its listeners. Both these rhythms and the rhythm of Hansen-Løve's film are being alluded to in its final scene where Robert Creeley's poem 'The Rhythm' is read by Paul (silently), and aloud in voiceover to the film's viewers.

Critical views among the French press of how successfully *Eden* conveys garage music's French proponents and followers differ, however, with *Cahiers du cinéma*'s Joachim Lepastier considering, in an article entitled 'Far from paradise', that in Paul Vallée's explanation that *Cheers*'s music aims at a mood 'between euphoria and melancholy', euphoria is very much the 'poor relation' of the pair (Lepastier 2014: 28). Lepastier sneers slightly at how the film's cast – Pauline Etienne as Louise, Laura Smet as Margot and Vincent Macaigne as Arnaud – were all extremely fashionable actors of the moment (2014: 28), as does D.F for *Le Canard enchaîné* who derides the film as 'desperately cool' (*branché*) (D.F. 2014). Thierry Gandillot, writing for *Les Echos*, thinks it drags through over-length, and Eric Libiot of *L'Express* thinks it lacks drama, is superficial, and has clearly been made just so that garage music's followers (and particularly Sven Hansen-Løve) can wallow in nostalgia (Libiot 2014). Strongly in favour of the film however, in addition to *Les Inrockuptibles*, is *Libération*, whose J.G. calls it a 'smoothly flowing fresco' that is the 'riskiest and probably the most beautiful film undertaken by Hansen-Løve to date as well as the most ambitious' (J.G. 2014). *Eden*'s generic distinctiveness amid what could otherwise be considered a very homogeneous body of work by Hansen-Løve – family and work-based dramas of sentiment – seems to have divided its critics along certain lines repeated from one reviewer to the next. The film's appeal everywhere it was released outside France (Brazil, the USA, Mexico, Japan, Argentina and Taiwan as well as eleven European countries) must have followed more from its function as a music documentary than its telling of the personal story of one DJ, but despite criticism from within France and outside it, it constitutes much more than a digression or a curiosity among Hansen-Løve's films, and should be considered on its own merits as well as for what it shares with her less generically distinctive productions.

Conclusion

To return now to the questions about Hansen-Løve's compilation scores raised earlier in the chapter, it was evident from those discussions of non-garage pop and folk music that she selects a great deal of music from the 1950s, 1960s and 1970s. Since her own comments about her choice of music reveal that she does not calculate at all carefully what the effects of a given song on her audience will be, it seems unwise to suggest that there is any deliberate evocation of time periods preceding the setting of the films themselves, which is not earlier than the 1990s in any instance. But pop music other than the contemporary dance music heard in *All Is Forgiven, Goodbye First Love* and *Maya* connotes decades well before the action it accompanies, and folk music like the Celtic songs of Matt McGinn and Rory and Alex McEwan tends by its nature to transcend particular time periods and societies, speaking of universal issues such as relationships of love and kin. To describe the feelings stimulated by such music, 'nostalgic' may be an exaggeration, but rather like François Truffaut's re-use of Maurice Jaubert's 1930s scores in the 1970s, Hansen-Løve's musical choices can certainly take her audience back to earlier times and grander sentiments than are suggested by what we are viewing. When 'Corrie Doon' strikes up as Pamela stands silently in an urban metro carriage, for example, it is a sense of centuries-old protective parental love for their children that takes over our emotional response mechanisms.

A parallel effect of the folk and classical music Hansen-Løve employs may stem from songs rarely being in the French language: 'A la claire fontaine' sung by Huppert in the final scene of *Things to Come* is an exception, but all the Celtic and contemporary folk songs heard in the earlier films are in English, and the Schubert songs heard in *Things to Come* and *Maya* are, obviously, in

German. In the instance of an intradiegetic performance such as Chemla's in *Maya*, the use of German is entirely in keeping with the socio-cultural context in which the performance takes place, but realism cannot account for any performative effects by Schubert's 'Auf dem Wasser zu singen' in *Things to Come*, the folk songs of Donovan and Woody Guthrie in the same film, and Violeta Parra's nostalgic Hispanic ballads in *Goodbye First Love*. Powrie comments in *Music in Contemporary French Cinema* that

> [i]n the absence of a study that would give us guidance on this issue [the use of English-language songs in French films], it is probably safe to assume, given the widespread dissemination of English songs and the use of English more broadly (on the Internet for example) that many listeners are likely to understand some English lyrics, and that younger listeners may well understand more of the lyrics. (Powrie 2017: 24)

Hansen-Løve's films may well appeal to young and middle-aged adults more familiar with English than other age groups, and a factor in audience comprehension of their songs not mentioned by Powrie is social class, where again it seems probable that because her films are about middle-class people and likely to attract middle-class audiences, many members of those audiences will be familiar with English, as well as with some German and/or Spanish. As Hansen-Løve herself emphasises, she does not usually select the songs for her films on account of their lyrics, and crudely 'applying' their meaning(s) to the narrative they accompany may even prove misleading, but at the very least, the occurrence of songs that are more often in languages other than French is further evidence of her contemporaneity and of the transnational character of her cinema.

A final question about how music tends to work in Hansen-Løve's films concerns its 'narrational force' or ability to push narrative action along, which she associates with composed rather than compilation film scores, and that she prefers to avoid for this reason. It is indeed difficult to think of examples of where music in her films works in this way, but one memorable sequence where wordless music – Irishman Patrick Street's instrumental version of 'Music for a Found Harmonium' – takes over from dialogue altogether occurs in the scene of swimming in the river Loire early in *Goodbye First Love*. Camille and Sullivan have argued and made up again, and are then filmed separately and together at the river, swimming and interacting playfully. 'Music for a Found Harmonium' follows a structure typical for folk music of repeated sequences whose intensity builds through additional instrumentation as well as volume, and features an accented, jaunty refrain to which rhythm and harmony are far more important than melody, with guitar and harmonium the main performers. Here, music does not push narrative along, because it is not advancing, in what is a perfect example of an interlude in narrative. Camille and Sullivan are at leisure, relaxing and playing, but these are actions that music can convey far better than words.

With the exception of *Eden*, music does not occupy a large proportion of any of Hansen-Løve's films, yet it is indispensable to all of them, fulfilling its conventional function of conveying mood and atmosphere and articulating characters' feelings as well as supplementing the expression of themes she has made her own – the coming-of-age of adolescent and young women, romantic love, its loss, and the difficulty of mourning it. As intimated in the section on Celtic folk music above, tracks such as Johnny Flynn and Laura Marling's 'The Water' in *Goodbye First Love* draw attention to music's reputation – along with film, perhaps – as an art of time, and the importance of time to Hansen-Løve's films is what I shall investigate in the next and final chapter.

Notes

All translations, unless otherwise stated, are the author's own.

1   Gorbman explains the ambiguity in the Afterword to her book, saying that the latter part of her title both 'restricts the investigation to *music for narrative films*' and 'refers to *music as a narrational force*' (both emphases original) (Gorbman 1987: 162).

2   Lorenz has come to the Ardèche with her, replacing Sullivan, and will join her outing shortly: can Camille therefore be said to be 'triumphantly alone'? (Handyside 2019: 14).

3   'Frank Sinatra 2001' was written by Caroline Hervé and Michel Amato, and 'Now That Love Is Gone' by Paul de Homem-Christo and Romain Céo.

4   'Que Sera Sera' was written by Jay Livingston and Ray Evans, and Doris Day performed it with Franck Devel & His Orchestra.

5   'Egyptian Reggae' was co-written by Earl Johnson and Jonathan Richman, 'South American Folk Song' by Richman alone.

6   The term 'chronicle' is also used of the film by Dominique Widermann in 'Mia Hansen-Løve fait sonner la fin de party', (Widermann 2014), and by Jean-Marc Lalanne in *Les Inrockuptibles* (Lalanne 2014a). An alternative genre suggested by Lalanne, who remarks that *Eden* takes in the great and the small while telling the 'collective and heroic adventure' of an entire generation of DJs, is the epic, albeit of an unspectacular kind (Lalanne 2014b).

7   Philippe Azoury emphasises the non- and even anti-commercial character of house and garage music, stating that brands, record companies and magazines were not interested in it, just the two Paris radio stations FG and Nova plus the occasional provincial network such as Montpellier's 'les Pingouins'. Three or four clubs, four record shops and one important journalist, Didier Lestrade of *Libération*, who wrote a column for its followers, were also interested in the movement (Azoury 2014).

6

The rivers of time

In an interview conducted at the 2012 Toronto International Film Festival, Hansen-Løve comments that manipulating the flow of time in film is so foreign to her that it would never occur to her to use a flashback.[1] For her (at least at that point in her career), time flows constantly and in one direction, like the waters of a river, recalling the pre-Socratic Greek philosopher Heraclitus's comment that we never step into the same river twice – or at least, if the river is the same on the second occasion, its waters are not.[2] Hansen-Løve may not be entirely endorsing Heraclitus's view that the world is constantly changing, to which his younger contemporary Parmenides's philosophy of the unity of Being is usually contrasted, but her films are indeed all about change(s) in the lives of her protagonists. There are striking similarities in the way time is deployed in her six films up to *Maya*: whereas *All Is Forgiven*, *Goodbye First Love* and *Eden* stretch out over periods of between eight and twenty-one years and *Father of My Children*, *Things to Come* and *Maya* take place over much shorter periods of around one year, all six films end with a moment at which the chief protagonist takes stock of where she or he is in their life as a result of the events we have witnessed during the film. Rather than manipulating time to construct an end-stopped narrative, Hansen-Løve lets us share her characters' world for a certain – often extended – period, and closes the film only when we have seen enough to understand the (usually transformative) effects that life-events have exerted upon them over that period.

In order to discuss this deceptively simple manner of 'organising' time in her films, this chapter will first introduce some film-philosophical and film-critical concepts and sources that will make the discussion possible – Henri Bergson's notion of *durée* (duration), Gilles Deleuze's concept of the time-image, derived in part from Bergson and developed in *Cinema 2: The Time-Image* (1989), and Matilda Mroz's study *Temporality and Film Analysis* (2012), in which she draws on both Bergson and Deleuze (as well as others) to analyse temporality in film. I shall then move on to analyse sequences from *Goodbye First Love* and *Maya* that convey the passing of time in a particular manner, to suggest what mode of realism Hansen-Løve may be said to be engaging in, and to discuss the privileging of particular moments in time at the end of each of her films, before concluding the chapter by returning to ethics – that is, the ethical implications of how time is deployed across Hansen-Løve's cinema.

De-spatialising time: Bergsonian *durée* and Deleuze's time-image

The forward flow of time in Hansen-Løve's films is often continuous, but as earlier chapters have shown, it is sometimes marked by striking ellipses or caesuras that follow separation or mental breakdown in the film's narrative – a gap of eight years in *All Is Forgiven* after Victor and Annette's marriage comes undone, and one of three years after Camille's suicide attempt in *Goodbye First Love*. (In *Father of My Children* Grégoire's suicide occurs at the exact midpoint of the film, dividing it into a very perceptible 'before' and 'after', although the action continues without a break amid his family's grief.) The sense one has of the shape of the narratives of *All Is Forgiven* and *Father of My Children* calls for description in spatio-material and even geographical terms: it is as if the fabric of the film is torn, or a chasm or gorge has opened up between its parts. This tendency to use spatial metaphors to describe temporal disjunction is remarked upon by many theorists of time including Bergson, and is an aspect Bergson sought to avoid when developing his concept of duration, first set out in the essay *Time and Free Will: Essay on the Immediate Data of Consciousness* (1910). As Mroz states at the start of her study of cinematic time, 'An interest in temporal flux perhaps leads one inevitably towards Bergsonian thought' (2012: 2), and even though Bergson in fact criticised film as projected by the Lumières' cinematograph (in *Creative Evolution* (1911)) for not displaying the continuity of duration, because it worked by using successive frames of spaces photographed at different moments, Mroz cites Marcel L'Herbier and Béla Balázs to show that Bergson's notion of duration was already in circulation in film criticism of the early to mid-twentieth century (2012: 20). She continues:

> Duration, wrote Bergson, 'is a continuity which is really lived, but which is artificially decomposed for the greater convenience of customary knowledge'. That is, we have acquired the habit of 'substituting for the true duration lived by consciousness, an homogenous and independent Time'. (Mroz 2012: 35)

'Homogenous and independent time' is spatialised, measurable time, the time of clocks that 'does not tell the truth of duration but creates an illusion of measurable, predictable time' (Mroz 2012: 35). This is opposed to time as it is lived by consciousness, the experience of lived or existential time that Bergson first conceptualised, in *durée*, at the end of the nineteenth century.

Despite the currency of Bergsonian duration in film criticism as well as in philosophy in the early and mid-twentieth century, however, it has been widely recognised in contemporary film philosophy that Deleuze's enormously influential *Cinema* books revived and extended Bergson's thinking following their publication in the 1980s. Mroz states, 'The way in which Bergsonian duration requires us to think beyond our dominant habits of representation, in which time is conceived in terms of space, was extremely significant for the development of Deleuze's thinking about cinema' (Mroz 2012: 36–7), and William Brown, in the chapter on time and temporalities in his study of digital cinema, *Supercinema* (2013), explicitly links Bergsonian duration to Deleuze's time-image:

> With the time-image we see a direct image of time, or of what Deleuze, after Henri Bergson, terms duration. In time-images, events unfold in 'real' times (and spaces), and as such time-image films can seem to have much 'empty' time (and space) within them, or moments in which little action seems to take place. (Brown 2013: 90)

How the second part of this observation relates to Hansen-Løve's often leisurely narratives is a point I shall return to later, but here I wish simply to explain why it is that Bergson's thinking has now largely given way to Deleuze's concept of the time-image in analyses of cinematic time. This concept cannot be understood except in relation to its opposite, the movement-image, and Brown provides an admirably clear overview of this pair of terms:

> The difference between the movement-image and the time-image is often explained as an historic one: the movement-image ends and the time-image begins at the end of the Second World War. It is sometimes explained as a geographical difference, between the movement-image (America) and the time-image (Europe). Furthermore, the movement-image is often characterized by classical narrative [...], while the time-image occurs in films that reject narrative, in particular the European/modernist *auteur* films of the 1950s onwards. (Brown 2013: 90)

Mroz's more expansive exposition of the movement-image reveals how Deleuze first arrived at the concept (and by implication also the concept of the time-image):

> In the opening pages of *Cinema 1*, Deleuze reiterates Bergson's distinction between 'concrete duration' and 'abstract time'. Movement cannot be equated with positions in space or instants of time, with what are termed 'immobile sections'. Such positions or instants correspond

to a notion of abstract time. Movement will always occur in a concrete duration, it cannot be divided or subdivided. Bergson, Deleuze notes, associated abstract time with 'the cinematographic illusion'. Deleuze, however, argues that while cinema does present immobile or instantaneous 'sections'(that is, images), it does not simply add movement to an image, 'it immediately gives us a movement-image. It does give us a section, but a section which is mobile, not an immobile section + abstract movement' [...] Deleuze thus uses Bergson to delineate instantaneous images or immobile sections, movement-images, or mobile sections of duration, and time-images that are 'beyond' movement itself. (Mroz 2012: 37)

This summary by Mroz of the tripartite framework of (im)mobility and time overlaid by Deleuze onto Bergson's thought will, like the binary distinction of the movement-image from the time-image, recur in subsequent sections of this chapter.

Flow, movement and time in *Goodbye First Love* and *Father of My Children*

One particular river – the Loire, filmed in *Goodbye First Love* – demonstrates that Hansen-Løve shares a Bergsonian understanding of the unidirectional flow of time, because (*pace* Heraclitus) Camille does indeed step into this river twice. On the second occasion, approximately eight years after the first, it both is and is not the same: she takes the same walk to get there and crosses the same bridge, where a sign again identifies the river (here in its higher reaches in the Ardèche) for the viewer. After scrambling down its banks she strips down to her swimsuit and carefully lays out a towel on which she leaves her clothes and shoes, weighting them down with stones but forgetting to do the same with the hat bought for her by Sullivan for their Ardèche holiday seen early in the film. The symbolic flight of the hat (representing Sullivan) out of her life ends the film visually, but it is the flow of the water also described in Johnny Flynn and Laura Marling's

Figure 6.1 Camille's hat floats away downstream at the end of *Goodbye First Love*

song 'The Water' that dominates thematically (Figure 6.1). Flow as a form of movement is echoed by the more fleeting appearance of rivers in other films, such as the Danube in *All Is Forgiven* and the Loire again (much farther along its course through France) in *Father of My Children*.

If Hansen-Løve seems keenly conscious of lived, existential *durée*, though, does this make her a filmmaker of the time-image rather than the movement-image? As a contemporary European auteur, this seems more likely than not, but we cannot ignore that moving bodies abound in her films – walking, bicycle-riding and moped-riding bodies as well as the drivers and passengers of cars. (Camille and Sullivan share a moped in *Goodbye First Love*, and in *Maya*, Gabriel and Maya rely entirely on mopeds to move locally around Goa.) In at least two memorable instances, a film is launched by rhythmically edited shots of a moving body – Sullivan cycling through the dawn at the start of *Goodbye First Love*, and Grégoire walking briskly through Parisian streets back to his car in *Father of My Children*. Quite unlike the more conventional establishing shots of Vienna seen at the start of *All Is Forgiven* (although a number of shots of the particular *quartier* of Paris are seen before the camera meets Grégoire exiting from a hotel), these two sequences of movement take us straight into the character's consciousness and lived experience: Sullivan has left Camille in bed to go and buy condoms, and we feel his keen desire to return to her intently, even if we do not instantly know the purpose of his ride. These two montages of movement – eight shots of Sullivan cycling and seven of Grégoire walking – may actually serve as excellent examples of both Bergson's duration and Deleuze's time-image, in that they are rhythmically presented direct images of time rather than movement-images that do no more than show actions that add up to a plot. Deleuze employs the acronym 'SAS' to describe 'humans who find a situation (S), who carry out actions (A), and who as a result change that situation (S)' (Deleuze 1986, quoted in Brown 2013: 90), and that is clearly not the kind of action going on in these sequences, which depict impatience and desire through movement rather than a situation undergoing transformation by means of human agency.

Time tunnels in *Goodbye First Love* and *Maya*

In mainstream narrative cinema such as Hollywood drama, a conventional way of presenting the passing of time is the 'tunnel', a sequence of usually short scenes with little or no dialogue and generally accompanied by music that serves to compress the action of a period of time. Perhaps unexpectedly, this device is also to be found in Hansen-Løve's cinema: one 'tunnel' occurs just after the main, three-year-long ellipsis of *Goodbye First Love*, between Camille's suicide attempt and her meeting with Lorenz, in a sequence of shots of Camille working as an usherette, presumably to earn money to put towards the architectural studies she is about to begin. She puts on the bright red and blue uniform and blonde wig provided and gets on with the job, while seeming to interact very little with the crowds attending the event, an enduring solitude emphasised when she brings a man back to her flat (presumably for the first time since Sullivan's desertion) but tells him she cannot be touched by or share a bed with him. According to Jacques Mandelbaum, this sequence of short scenes is actually an inverted 'tunnel', since rather than compressing action in order to move on to the next 'act' of the film (which in Mandelbaum's view has three, in 1999, 2003 and 2007), it 'dilates' or opens time up, the film 'formally espousing Camille's state of mind' (Mandelbaum 2011) by showing us how immersing herself in work is gradually freeing her from the past.

A much more conventional use of a tunnel occurs in *Maya* as Gabriel makes the trip around India that is part of the *raison d'être* for his stay in the country: in a four-minute section of the film in which shots are often superimposed over a map and are accompanied by the arrangement for guitar of the Schubert serenade sung by Naomi early in the film, we see Gabriel on trains, in a taxi, getting on a tram, walking through brightly coloured markets, getting a shave at a barber's, interacting with local people, appreciating architecture, buying books and food, and sleeping. Although there is no dialogue except the odd unanswered remark during this sequence, the ambient sound of streets and parks continues beneath the lilting, melancholy music that exactly matches Gabriel's apparent mood. Despite conforming entirely conventionally to the compression of time (a period of several weeks) effected by a tunnel, this sequence also offers glimpses of a much wider variety of Indian urban civilisation than is seen in the Goa-based majority of *Maya*, and adds up to a kind of delicately constructed and orchestrated interlude in the film.

From narrative to phenomenological realism

The title of Florence Maillard's review of *Goodbye First Love*, 'The Time of Feeling' [*Le temps des sentiments*] (Maillard 2011) exactly echoes my exposition above of the Bergsonian character of Hansen-Løve's cinema – that time in her films is lived and subjective more than it is the measured, divisible, 'objective' time of clocks. Maillard, however, is more interested in the type of narrative this gives rise to than in any philosophical account of types of time, and in words that might refer to more of Hansen-Løve's films than just the one she is reviewing, describes *Goodbye First Love* as follows:

> The narrative never plays the card of opposing different time periods, dramatic interludes, heightened emotions or sentimental imbroglio. Patiently and chronologically, it inscribes events into a continuum [*durée*] and captures a progression – a movement that incorporates each person's solitude within a network of relationships [...] The look directed at characters is candid, direct, attentive and welcoming, and brings forth a kind of loose complexity from this flux [*écoulement*], which itself seems to accompany the flow of the seasons and to resonate with vibrations and variations in the brightness of the light. (Maillard 2011: 51)

Here Maillard captures brilliantly the characteristic pace of Hansen-Løve's films, which are leisurely in a way that clearly irritates some reviewers,[3] never hurried but simply concerned to set out steadily and chronologically what they have to show. *Télérama* critic Jacques Morice corroborates Maillard's observations when he describes *Goodbye First Love* as possessing 'a strange temporality, a sort of timeless present in which her characters evolve' (Morice 2011) – and comments, too, that this way of treating time is a kind of synthesis of the approaches of Truffaut and the 'post-New Wave' filmmakers Jean Eustache and Philippe Garrel, to both of whom Hansen-Løve is regularly compared by French critics.

Where does this very singular treatment of time, temporality and pace leave Hansen-Løve's filmmaking among modes of realism? (a category of fiction into which it does fall, even if the term does not particularly enhance our understanding of it). Despite regular sharp observations about the contemporary neoliberal era – the practices of unscrupulous Indian property developers (*Maya*), or the marketisation of academic publishing (*Things to Come*) – her filmmaking is not social realism. Nor is it narrative realism of the kind in which different plotlines are drawn together into satisfying finality, as the films do not really deal in levels of plot at all, despite evidently being concerned with a sequence of events. The motor force of the films is feeling or sentiment rather than the type of action referred to by Deleuze's movement-image or SAS acronym. They last just as long as the protagonist(s) need to get through the adversity confronting them, and Hansen-Løve's interest in people and subjectivity outweighs her interest in action and narrative.[4] I would suggest therefore that she could be termed a phenomenological realist, concerned above all to offer visual 'descriptions' of the world and her characters' experiences of it. The phenomenology undertaken by Hansen-Løve's camera is not the methodical description of Husserlian phenomenologists, but something like the 'spiritual seeing'[5] described by Max Scheler (the philosopher on whom she wrote her dissertation), a loving attitude able to penetrate to layers of sentiment that are invisible to casual observation. Hansen-Løve certainly makes images of the world that may broadly be termed 'realistic', but she is interested above all in the description of human feeling that moves and motivates her characters on their personal journeys.[6]

Moments in time

Mroz begins the 'Moments and Duration' section of the introductory chapter of *Temporality and Film Analysis* by saying: 'Definitions, descriptions and theorisations of film moments can be found throughout the history of writing on film' (Mroz 2012: 34). There are a great variety of such moments in films and in writing about films, she then adds, 'a moment of pure sensation, as in Sobchack's writing, or a moment which has a "cue" attached to it, as in cognitive theory' (2012: 35). Without preferring one theoretical or philosophical account of film moments to another, I would like now to comment on the privileged moments that occur at the end of each of Hansen-Løve's films – or at least at the end of *Father of My Children* and *Eden*, since the endings of *All Is Forgiven*, *Goodbye First Love*, *Things to Come* and *Maya* have been discussed in previous chapters or earlier in this one.

It may be that the mood of relaxed equanimity resounding through Doris Day's singing of 'Que Sera Sera' is what stays with the viewer with respect to the final moments of *Father of My Children*, and this hopeful resignation is an important part of the film's conclusion. Given that what we are watching are the three Canvel daughters and their mother in a taxi at the start of their first holiday since Grégoire's suicide, it is significant that the voice of the song is a woman remembering counsel from her mother and her 'sweetheart' to accept what the future will bring, then passing on the same advice to her own children, exactly matching Sylvia's situation as a mother, and chiming with the theme of filiation emphasised in Arthur Malkavian's film *Families of Chance*, the script of which Valentine has just come across in Grégoire's office.[7] Before 'Que Sera Sera' strikes up, however, the atmosphere in the taxi is sober, with nobody speaking until Billie cheerfully calls out 'Goodbye Paris!', which causes Clémence to cry. Fighting back sobs and wiping away tears, Clémence reminds her mother and sisters that they had said they would return to Grégoire's grave before leaving Paris, a visit Sylvia replies that they no longer have the time to make. But Sylvia's remark is not made unfeelingly and reminds us that the film itself has not visited the cemetery where Grégoire is buried, emphasising the extent to which its second half is identified with the time and continuing lives of those who have survived him.

The closing moments of *Eden* draw attention to a similar combination of retrospection and contemplation of the future. Paul is alone in his flat having just returned from one of the writing workshops he is now attending, where he has been befriended by a young woman called Estelle (Olivia Ross). Estelle has caught up with Paul in the street after leaving the class in order to lend him a collection of Robert Creeley's poems entitled 'The End', in which she has marked one poem in particular that reminds her of Paul. As Paul, who is already familiar with Creeley's writings, opens the book to read 'The Rhythm', Estelle's voice is heard in voiceover reading it, and her image appears superimposed on the one of Paul lying on his bed reading, as the poem's words fade in and out on the screen, one verse at a time:

> It is all a rhythm,
> from the shutting
> door, to the window
> opening,
>
> […]
>
> The rhythm which projects
> from itself continuity
> bending all to its force
> from window to door,
> from ceiling to floor,
> light at the opening,
> dark at the closing.

The poem's sombre last couplet is matched by Paul's expression as he takes it in, but more striking in these final seconds of the film is the multi-layered, constantly shifting composition of the image – a fine example of a Deleuzian time-image, which combines silent reading and contemplation that the viewer is invited to share via the on-screen text with a rhythmic presentation of that text both visually and aurally. Hansen-Løve comments on her 'obsession' with rhythm in the interview for *The Seventh Art* cited at the start of this chapter, and closing *Eden* with a reading of a poem entitled 'The Rhythm' is both a highly appropriate ending to a film built around the hypnotically pulsating beat of EDM (electronic dance music, as house and garage are also known) and an echo of the rhythms of feeling that structure all Hansen-Løve's films, where grief and mourning are repeatedly counterbalanced by more buoyant currents of emotion.[8]

Conclusion: the ethics of *durée*

I concluded Chapter 1's exploration of *fracture familiale* in Hansen-Løve's cinema by suggesting that the focus of her first three films on adolescent girl characters 'signals an ethical openness to modifiability and the future'. In this chapter, it has become evident that such an openness is also at work in the way time is deployed in her films: their concluding scenes repeatedly show the protagonists at moments in their lives that are significant because they point forwards as well as back (*Father of My Children, Goodbye First Love, Maya*) or explicitly refer to aspects of temporality such as rhythm (*Eden* and *Things to Come*, where the words of 'Unchained Melody' include 'time goes by so slowly, and time can do so much'). At these moments as well as in the empathy with her characters that prevails over narrative in Hansen-Løve's films, time overflows the present in the manner characteristic of Bergsonian duration. It is therefore revealing to note that Bergson's commentators have observed the ethical content of the very concept of *durée*, and that Levinas, the philosopher of ethics who is one of the sources of Butler's writings on precariousness and vulnerability drawn on in Chapters 1 and 2, frequently credits Bergson as an ethical thinker.

In the chapter of his 1999 study of Bergson titled 'The Ethics of Durée', John Mullarkey comments:

> That Bergson's work is driven by ethical motives certainly seems confirmed when one reads him making pronouncements such that, for him, 'automatism is the enemy'. But TSMR [*The Two Sources of Morality and Religion* [1932]] has added a new dimension to this ethical enterprise. By writing of an ethical emotion – openness or love – which is 'more metaphysical than moral in its essence', it looks as though his thought may not merely be animated by a certain moral outrage, but that ethics itself may comprise its content in some form. As we put it in our introduction: Bergsonism may best be read as an ethics of alterity fleshed out in empirical concerns. (Mullarkey 1999: 106–7)

Mullarkey's mention here of an ethics of alterity (a reference to Levinas in all but name) is followed by a quotation from Levinas's essay 'The Old and the New' in which Levinas, lecturing in 1979/80, insists 'on the importance of Bergsonism for the entire problematic of contemporary philosophy' (Levinas, quoted in Mullarkey 1999: 109). This is because Bergson's prioritising of duration over permanence offers 'access to novelty, an access independent of the ontology of the Same' (1999: 109). Bergson's privileging of lived, subjective time over the mechanical time of clocks entails the same kind of reversal as Levinas's privileging of ethics over ontology, in his understanding of ethics as 'first philosophy'. Indeed, after the publication of his second major work *Otherwise than Being* in 1974, Levinas drew attention to the importance of Bergson's thought not just in 'The Old and the New', but in 'Death and Time', a lecture series given in 1976 and later published in English in a volume entitled *God, Death and Time* (Levinas 1993).[9] Here, Levinas finds in Heidegger a similar idea of different levels of time as is articulated by Bergson in *durée* – '[o]riginary time he calls *duration*; this is a becoming in which each instant is heavy with all of the past and pregnant with the whole future' (Levinas 1993: 55) – and implies a preference for Bergson's approach to time and death over Heidegger's. Levinas also points out in 'Death and Time' that duration, initially set out in *Time and Free Will* (1910) and *Creative Evolution* (1911), undergoes further development in Bergson's late work *The Two Sources of Morality and Religion* (1935), where it becomes the explicitly ethical 'interhuman life', 'the fact that a man can appeal to the interiority of another man' (Levinas 1993: 55–6). Bearing out Mullarkey's views that 'Bergson's work is driven by ethical motives' and that 'his thought may not merely be animated by a certain moral outrage, but that ethics itself may comprise its content in some form', these approving references to Bergson by Levinas strongly indicate the relevance of ethics to Bergson's philosophy of time and concept of *durée*.

The purpose of the short digression above into intersections of time and ethics in philosophy was to return to and pick up the arguments advanced in my discussions of precarious families, vulnerability and work-as-vocation in Chapters 1, 2 and 3 and link them to the way in which time is deployed in Hansen-Løve's cinema. This chapter has argued that for Hansen-Løve, time is a unidirectional flow akin to Bergsonian *durée*, that her films offer many examples of the rhythmically presented direct images of time theorised by Deleuze in *Cinema 2: The Time-Image*, and that this understanding and presentation of time as lived, existential and subjective is ethical by its very nature. I shall now move on to draw some general conclusions that arise from all six chapters of the book, returning as I do so to the questions raised in the introduction about Hansen-Løve's status as a young, female auteur working in France but already possessing an established international reputation.

Notes

All translations, unless otherwise stated, are the author's own.

1   This interview was carried out by Christopher Heron for *The Seventh Art*, and can be viewed at <https://www.youtube.com/watch?v=z_ UWnuqa1Yk>

2   Heraclitus of Ephesus (530–470 BC) made this comment in three separate fragments, B12, B49a and B91, of which B49a, 'We both step and do not step in the same rivers. We are and are not', is generally considered the most authentic. The river is evidently being employed as a metaphor for the nature of Being, or reality.

3   Thierry Gandillot's view of *Eden* (Hansen-Løve's longest film) is that it drags because its screenplay is too thin (see 'Les souffrances du jeune raveur' in *Les Echos*, 19 November 2014): the alternative point of view is put by Serge Kaganski for *Les Inrocks* when he says 'It is precisely its length [*durée*] which gives the film its strength and beauty – its density [*épaisseur*] and meaning', *Les Inrockuptibles* 19 November 2014.

4   Maillard's commentary on the relationship between narrative and character in the films supports this: 'It's not so much that they [the characters] lead the narrative: they are ahead of it, they outmanoeuvre it, they are always already elsewhere. In a way, they are superior to it, or foreign to it; they are not caught up in its machinery' (Maillard 2011: 51).

5   Scheler (1973), p. 137.

6   On realism, Hansen-Løve has the following to say: 'I don't believe in realism. When people tell me "your movies are realist" then I can say that yes, it's true that I try to give a sense of reality. I try to make it so that people have this feeling of a cinema that is real. However, it is not the reality as it is that interests me . . . That's why when I hear the word "realism" it always makes me feel weird because yes, my cinema is apparently completely anchored in reality but what interests me is something that goes above and beyond the surface' (Ganjavie 2016: 9).

7   This contemplation of the future made possible by filiation is also seen at the end of *All Is Forgiven*, where the sentiments of the von Eichendorff poem Victor wrote out to send to Pamela just before he died, and that she reads aloud to Judith as they leave his funeral (once she has translated the German into French), emphasise wariness, alertness and spirited energy (its closing line is 'Be wary, stay alert and full of gusto' ['Prends garde, reste alerte et plein d'entrain']).

8   Hansen-Løve's comment is that she is 'obsessed' by rhythm in a way she imagines many filmmakers are, particularly as it relates to the transitions crafted when editing. Christopher Heron's interview with her for *The Seventh Art* is at <https://www.youtube.com/watch?v=z_UWnuqa1Yk>

9   The chapter was published first in *La Mort et le Temps* (Levinas 1991), the English translation of which appears with a second lecture, 'God and Philosophy', in *God, Death and Time*.

Conclusion: contemporaneity and the ethic of transcendence

An aspect of Hansen-Løve's films I have mentioned but not explored in the chapters of this book is the contemporaneity and precise dating of their action: *All Is Forgiven* takes place in 1995–6 and 2007, *Father of My Children* in the mid-2000s when Humbert Balsan took his own life, *Goodbye First Love* between 1999 and 2007, *Eden* between 1992 and 2013, *Things to Come* during Nicolas Sarkozy's presidency of 2007 to 2012, and *Maya* in 2012–13, early in François Hollande's presidential term. The French political context of the period or moment of the films' action is of little importance in the first four, but more significant in *Things to Come*, because of the strike seen at Nathalie Chazeaux's high school and the intellectual differences between Nathalie and her anarchist former pupil Fabien, and in *Maya*. As Richard Porton observes of *Things to Come* in his second article-interview with Hansen-Løve for *Cinéaste*:

> In any case, the allusions to intellectual heavyweights do not constitute mere name-dropping. Nathalie's investment in Adorno and Horkheimer's pessimistic brand of Marxism provides her with a radical scepticism that helps her to ward off some of her students' more naïve provocations and mordantly conclude that even her own intellectual efforts are subject to the whims of the culture industry. (Porton 2017: 24)

Differences between Nathalie and Fabien that emerge during her first visit to the 'oddly idyllic anarchist commune' (Porton

2017: 24) where he lives draw on actual political debates of 2007:

> Nathalie is not particularly convinced by the group's advocacy of anonymous political interventions, a precept borrowed from the activities of the 'Invisible Committee', a group whose 2007 post-Situationist manifesto, 'The Coming Insurrection', enraged conservatives who believed it was less a theoretical text than a rationalization for terrorism and sabotage. (Porton 2017: 24)

Nathalie's investment in traditional forms of Marxism, described by Porton as 'proudly bourgeois radicalism' (2017: 24) does nonetheless point up Hansen-Løve's awareness of the importance to contemporary France of regretful former Communists, the factuality of which Porton asks her about in the interview:

> Yes, I think it's the story of a lot of intellectuals in France today … Discussions between communists and *gauchistes*, leftists who were never communists, comprise an important part of intellectual debate in contemporary France. There are still conflicts between these unapologetic Stalinists, repentant communists, and leftists who assail the Stalinist past. This divide is a big part of the French intellectual landscape and explains, to a certain extent, why the French left is so weak now. / This is not what the film is about, but I felt I had to depict these conflicts in a very precise way … I don't agree with the assumption that, because it's cinema, you have to simplify complex political debates. That was part of the challenge of conveying these debates on screen. (Porton 2017: 26)

The same political and historical precision Hansen-Løve registers in *Things to Come* – and which she believes cinema can transmit – can be seen in *Maya*'s treatment of the issue of French journalists taken hostage in the Middle East. Interestingly, it is again in the relationship between a young man and a mature woman – Gabriel and his mother – that differences surface, since, in their sole conversation in Mumbai, Johanna is bitterly critical of how the French government has funds for the release of hostages that it does not draw on for international aid to support refugees and street children, an inequality briefly glimpsed in the film's prologue when money exchanges hands as Gabriel and Frédéric readjust to Parisian life after their ordeal.

A further exact depiction by Hansen-Løve of a historico-political trend can be seen in the resilience her protagonists develop through the ethic of vocation discussed in Chapter 3. As a term, 'resilience' has become increasingly prevalent over the decades in which neoliberalism has become hegemonic, with the theme of the 'resilient self' treated in an industry of self-help books that 'became a technology of neoliberal government' (Bracke 2016: 53). Hansen-Løve's protagonists are not readers of the kind of resilience discourse propagated by self-help books, so Sarah Bracke's observation that 'the idea of resilience as a personal virtue now reaches far beyond the readership of such self-help books. Resilience, we could argue, has become a force to be reckoned with in the realm of hegemonic ethics of and truths about the self' (2016: 53) is more pertinent to the films treated in Chapter 3 than the neoliberal theme of the 'resilient self'. For Camille of *Goodbye First Love*, whose career in architecture sustains her personally as well as professionally, through her relationship with Lorenz, resilience is progressively discovered rather than acquired, but by the films of the second half of the 2010s, the protagonists' resilience has become more like the kind demanded and promoted by neoliberal economics and ideology. Nathalie Chazeaux, who exhibits it more than any other character, has her children as well as her profession to sustain her through the transformation of her lifestyle brought by divorce, but the recovery and return to work of Gabriel Dahan – who 'bounces back' in just the manner referred to by many commentators on resilience – inhibits and diminishes his relationships with others, as Maya is only too aware.

Noting how Hansen-Løve's depiction of female characters has developed since the set of three films about young and adolescent girls with which she made her name allows me to return to the issues of gender representation and (gendered) authorship discussed in the introduction to and Chapter 2 of this book. The characters of Paul's mother in *Eden* and Nathalie of *Things to Come* have added two remarkable older women to the girls whose autonomy is emphasised by Emma Wilson and Fiona Handyside, whereas *Maya*'s eponymous protagonist presents viewers with a further girl-woman, this time one whose independence is in tension with her lover's privileging of his work over his personal life and with her overprotective father's insistence on her education. The setting of *Maya* in Anglophone India makes the film more comparable than earlier ones to Sofia Coppola's 'Nameless Trilogy' of girlhood films with which Handyside pairs Hansen-Løve's trilogy (Handyside 2015), employing Rosalind Gill's work on postfeminist media culture to draw out the similarities between the two directors. Insofar as Hansen-Løve's films circulate in some of the same festival and exhibition circuits as Coppola's, her parallel is entirely valid, although it seems to me that Hansen-Løve acknowledged her first three films to be a trilogy when the Toronto International Film Festival screened them together in a mini-retrospective in 2012 rather than ever declaring, 'labelling' or 'proclaiming' them to be one (2015: 1, 9).[1] Gill's identification of postfeminism as a cultural sensibility (2007) certainly seems relevant to Hansen-Løve's girl characters, as Handyside asserts by saying that '[t]he girl coming of age can thus be considered as a representative figure of postfeminist values' (Handyside 2015: 4), but since Hansen-Løve's base in Paris is unlikely to expose her to Anglophone academic writing on postfeminist media culture or to very many of that culture's media products, and she has gone along with the suggestion that her first three films form a loose trilogy rather than actively promoting the fact, I am sceptical of '[t]he self-conscious declaration of agency and authorship via the promotion of the trilogy' (2015: 5) that Handyside claims for her, which may well be more justified where Coppola is concerned. I do not think this 'very particular claiming of the power of authorship' (2015: 5) that Handyside reads 'as self-consciously repudiating a feminist position' (2015: 5) should be attributed to Hansen-Løve: if 'postfeminist' is employed 'in the sense of benefitting from and enriching feminist insights' (2015: 5), as Handyside employs it, acknowledging that 'such entangled feminist and antifeminist ideas are typical of postfeminist cultural production' (2015: 5), the term is doing little work apart from placing Hansen-Løve in her context as a twenty-first-century filmmaker. As I argued when discussing Hansen-Løve's identity as an auteur in the introduction to this book, her reluctance to situate herself as a female auteur arises from the French context in which she works rather than from any repudiation of feminism, even while she has (from 2016 onwards) increasingly pursued English-language production and continued the 'savvy navigation of . . . production context' (2015: 10) that Handyside observes her to have undertaken in France for the first decade of her career. Hansen-Løve's seventh film, *Bergman Island* (forthcoming, 2021), is an English-language production in which the Australian and American actors Mia Wasikowska and Tim Roth take the starring roles, accompanied by Luxembourgian actress Vicky Krieps and a number of other European, American and dual-national actors. Its combination of performers from three different continents and a setting on the Swedish island of Fårö, where Ingmar Bergman lived and is buried, seems set to further complicate questions about different cultural influences on her filmmaking.

In Chapters 3 and 4 I explored first the ethical then the aesthetic dimension of Hansen-Løve's evident interest in experiences of transcendence, emphasising the philosophical understanding of cinema she seems to have developed out of the influence of her philosopher-teacher parents and her own study of the subject. An interview about *Things to Come* that Hansen-Løve gave to the magazine section of the streaming service MUBI confirms the relevance of philosophy to her filmmaking, less because of her study of it (she claims no 'real knowledge or mastery of philosophy' (Ganjavie 2016: 4)) than because of her own intuition (ironically, a concept dear to German phenomenology) and her parents' influence:

> I grew up in a world where from a very young age, I was repeatedly told that philosophy was love and wisdom, and that the important thing in life was to find the right sense and to search for beauty, for goodness, and to try to understand what was good and right. (Ganjavie 2016: 4)

The search for wisdom, the good and beauty that philosophy represented for her parents transferred itself to Hansen-Løve and to her filmmaking:

> Finally, for me, cinema is nothing but another way to practice philosophy … Philosophy is philosophy and cinema is cinema but it is true that for me, at least, it is the only way; it is my way to handle these questions. (Ganjavie 2016: 5)

Hansen-Løve seems to concede that this way of working is idealistic without using the word when she adds that it engages her (or any artist adopting it) in an 'infinite' search (Ganjavie 2016: 9). Rather than criticise her possible idealism, however, I want to re-emphasise the connection between this way of working and the philosophical and theological tendencies of her films brought out in Chapters 3 and 4. The post-secular faith that Hansen-Løve's protagonists have in their work, the experiences of transcendence they undergo in the beauty of Nature, in romantic and family love, and in music, her admiration for the 'mystery' of Rohmer's cinema and her esteem for Bresson's all point to what I shall call her ethic of transcendence, which she actually articulates in the interview with MUBI quoted above after explaining how she sought, when making *Things to Come*, to bring out recently overlooked aspects of Isabelle Huppert's performance style. To the interviewer's suggestion that she 'searched for transcendence in the ordinary' (2016: 9), Hansen-Løve replies, 'Yes, exactly, but I'm also looking to say it in another way, I look for the invisible in the real … What interests me is not to reproduce the real but to transmit a feeling of invisibility' (2016: 9).

This feeling of invisibility or mystery that Hansen-Løve seeks to convey in her cinema is not Rohmer's or Bresson's but her own, a twenty-first-century ethic of transcendence, and a central element of the approach to character portrayal, narrative and aesthetics that together make up her singular film-making style.

Note

1   Handyside does also refer to both Coppola's and Hansen-Løve's trilogies as 'accidental' trilogies in that they were 'designated as such only after the third film had been made' (Handyside 2015: 1–2).

Bibliography

Bauman, Zygmunt (2000), *Liquid Modernity*, Oxford and Malden, MA: Polity Press.

Bauman, Zygmunt (2003), *Liquid Love: on the Frailty of Human Bonds*, Oxford and Malden, MA: Polity Press.

Bergson, Henri (1910 [1889]), *Time and Free Will: Essay on the Immediate Data of Consciousness*, authorised translation by F. L. Pogson, London: Allen & Unwin.

Bergson, Henri (1911 [1907]), *Creative Evolution*, authorised translation by Arthur Mitchell, London: Macmillan.

Bergson, Henri (1935 [1932]), *The Two Sources of Morality and Religion*, trans. R. Ashley Audra and Cloudesley Brereton, with the assistance of W. Horsfall Carter, London: Macmillan.

Blanchard, Pascal, Nicolas Bancel and Sandrine Lemaire (2006), *La fracture coloniale: la société française au prisme de l'héritage colonial*, Paris: La Découverte.

Bracke, Sarah (2016), 'Bouncing Back: Vulnerability and Resistance in Times of Resilience', in Judith Butler, Zeynap Gambetti and Leticia Sorbsay (eds), *Vulnerability in Resistance*, Durham, NC: Duke University Press, pp. 52–75.

Brown, William (2013), *Supercinema: Film-Philosophy for the Digital Age*, New York and Oxford: Berghahn Books.

Butler, Judith (2000a), 'Politics, Power and Ethics: a Discussion between Judith Butler and William Connolly', *Theory & Event* 4: 2. Available at: <https://www.muse.jhu.edu/article/32589> (last accessed 1 June 2019).

Butler, Judith (2000b), 'Ethical Ambivalence', in Marjorie Garber, Beatrice Hanssen and Rebecca L. Walkowitz (eds), *The Turn to Ethics*, New York: Routledge, pp. 15–28.

Butler, Judith (2004), *Precarious Life: The Powers of Mourning and Violence*, London and New York: Verso.

Butler, Judith (2005), *Giving an Account of Oneself*, New York: Fordham University Press.

Butler, Judith (2010), *Frames of War. When Is Life Grievable?*, London and New York: Verso.

Butler, Judith (2012), *Parting Ways: Jewishness and the Critique of Zionism*, New York: Columbia University Press.

Butler, Judith (2015), *Senses of the Subject*, New York: Fordham University Press.

Cooke, Mervyn (2008), *A History of Film Music*, Cambridge: Cambridge University Press.

Critchley, Simon (2012), *Infinitely Demanding: Ethics of Commitment, Politics of Resistance*, London and New York: Verso.

Deleuze, Gilles (1989), *Cinema 2: The Time-Image*, trans. Hugh Tomlinson and Robert Galeta, London: Athlone.

Delorme, Stéphane (2011), 'La source cachée', interview with Mia Hansen-Løve in *Cahiers du cinéma* 668 (June), 52–4.

Fineman, Martha A. (2004), *The Autonomy Myth: A Theory of Dependency*, New York: The New Press.

Fineman, Martha A. (2008) 'The Vulnerable Subject: Anchoring Equality in the Human Condition', *Yale Journal of Law & Feminism* 20: 1, 1–23.

Fineman, Martha A. and Anna Grear (eds) (2016), *Vulnerability: Reflections on a New Ethical Foundation for Law and Politics*, London and New York: Routledge.

Flood, Maria (2018), '"The Very Worst Things": Violence and Vulnerability in Djamila Sahraoui's *Yema* (2012)', *Studies in French Cinema* 19: 3, 246–64.

Frodon, Jean-Michel (2009), 'Le cinéma, c'était ça', *Cahiers du cinéma* 645 (May), p. 28.

Ganjavie, Amir (2016), 'Can Philosophy Save Your Life? An Interview with Mia Hansen- Løve', MUBI Notebook Interview, 18 December. Available at: <https://mubi.com/notebook/posts/can-philosophy-save-your-life-an-interview-with-mia-hansen-love> (last accessed 1 April 2020).

Gill, Rosalind (2007), 'Postfeminist Media Culture: Elements of a Sensibility', *European Journal of Cultural Studies* 10: 2, 147–66.

Gorbman, Claudia (1987), *Unheard Melodies: Narrative Film Music*, London: British Film Institute.

Habermas, Jürgen (2008), 'Secularism's Crisis of Faith: Notes on Post-Secular Society', *New Perspectives Quarterly* 25: 4 (Fall), 17–29.

Handyside, Fiona (2015), 'Girlhood, Postfeminism and Contemporary Female Art-House Authorship: The "Nameless Trilogies" of Sofia Coppola and Mia Hansen- Løve', *Alphaville: Journal of Film and Screen Media* 10 (Winter).

Handyside, Fiona (2016), 'Emotion, Girlhood, and Music in *Naissance des pieuvres* (Céline Sciamma, 2007) and *Un amour de jeunesse* (Mia Hansen-Løve, 2011)', in Fiona Handyside and Kate Taylor-Jones (eds),

International Cinema and the Girl: Local Issues, Transnational Contexts, London and New York: Palgrave Macmillan, pp. 121–33.

Handyside, Fiona (2019), 'Words for a Conversation: Speech, Doubt and Faith in the Films of Eric Rohmer and Mia Hansen-Løve', *Studies in French Cinema* 19: 1, 5–21.

Hansen-Løve, Mia (2012), 'Nous, les femmes', *Cahiers du cinéma* 681 (September), 28–9.

Heron, Christopher (2012), interview with Mia Hansen-Løve, *The Seventh Art*. Available at: <https://www.youtube.com/watch?v=z_UWnuqa1Yk> (last accessed 10 March 2020).

Jones, Kristin M. (2010), 'Now and Forever: Family Ties Unravel in the Films of Mia Hansen-Løve', *Film Comment* 46: 3 (May/June), 56.

Jones, Kristin M. (2015), review of *Eden*, *Film Comment* 51: 3 (May/June), 67–8.

Kalinak, Kathryn (2010), *Film Music: A Very Short Introduction*, Oxford: Oxford University Press.

Kelly, Casey Ryan (2017), '*It Follows*: Precarity, Thanatopolitics, and the Ambient Horror Film', *Critical Studies in Media Communication* 34: 3, 234–49.

King, Gemma (2017), *Decentering France: Multilingualism and Power in Contemporary French Cinema*, Manchester: Manchester University Press.

Kristeva, Julia (2010), 'Liberty, Equality, Fraternity . . . and Vulnerability', trans. Jeanine Herman in *WSQ: Women's Studies Quarterly* 38: 1–2, 251–68.

Levinas, Emmanuel (1987), 'The Old and the New', in *Time and the Other* [and additional essays], trans. Richard A. Cohen, Pittsburgh, PA: Duquesne University Press, pp. 128–38.

Levinas, Emmanuel (1993), *God, Death and Time*, trans. Bettina Burgo, Stanford, CA: Stanford University Press.

Lloyd, Moya (2008), 'Towards a Cultural Politics of Vulnerability: Precarious Lives and Ungrievable Deaths', in Terrell Carver and Samuel A. Chambers (eds), *Judith Butler's Precarious Politics: Critical Encounters*, London and New York: Routledge, pp. 92–106.

Lloyd, Moya (2015), *Butler and Ethics*, Edinburgh: Edinburgh University Press.

Lübecker, Nikolaj (2015), *The Feel-Bad Film*, Edinburgh: Edinburgh University Press.

Mackenzie, Catriona, Wendy Rogers and Susan Dodds (eds) (2014), *Vulnerability: New Essays in Ethics and Feminist Philosophy*, Oxford: Oxford University Press.

Mera, Miguel and David Burnand (eds) (2006), *European Film Music*, Aldershot and Burlington, VT: Ashgate Publishing Ltd.

Mroz, Matilda (2012), *Temporality and Film Analysis*, Edinburgh: Edinburgh University Press.

Mullarkey, John (1999), *Bergson and Philosophy*, Edinburgh: Edinburgh University Press.

O'Connor, Rory (2016), 'Mia Hansen-Løve on the Precision of Isabelle Huppert and the Simplicity of *Things to Come*', *The Film Stage*, 17 February. Available at: <https://thefilmstage.com/features/mia-hansen-love-on-the-precision-of-isabelle-huppert-and-the-simplicity-of-things-to-come> (last accessed 20 September 2018).

Porton, Richard (2010), 'A Death in the Family: an Interview with Mia Hansen-Løve', *Cinéaste* 35: 3 (Summer), 10–14.

Porton, Richard (2017), 'Love, Work and Radical Ideals: an Interview with Mia Hansen-Løve', *Cineaste* 42: 2 (Spring), 24–7.

Powrie, Phil (1997), *French Cinema in the 1980s: Nostalgia and the Crisis of Masculinity*, Oxford: Oxford University Press.

Powrie, Phil (2017), *Music in Contemporary French Cinema: The Crystal-Song*, Cham: Palgrave Macmillan/Springer International Publishing AG.

Pudlowski, Charlotte (2012), 'Le Cinéma français est-il misogyne?', *Slate.fr*, 23 May. Available at: <http://www.slate.fr/story/56429/cinema-francais-misogyne> (last accessed 31 December 2012).

Ratti, Manav (2013), *The Postsecular Imagination: Postcolonialism, Religion and Literature*, London and New York: Routledge.

Schehr, Lawrence R. (2009), *French Post-Modern Masculinities: From Neuromatrices to Seropositivity*, Liverpool: Liverpool University Press.

Scheler, Max (1973), *Selected Philosophical Essays*, trans. David Lachterman, Evanston, IL: Northwestern University Press.

Schrader, Paul (1972), *Transcendental Style in Film: Ozu, Bresson, Dreyer*, Berkeley, CA: University of California Press.

Sellier, Geneviève (2015), 'Pitiful Men, Instrumental Women: the Reconfiguration of Masculine Domination in Contemporary Popular French Cinema', in Alistair Fox, Michel Marie, Raphaëlle Moine and Hilary Radner (eds), *A Companion to Contemporary French Cinema*, Chichester: Wiley Blackwell, pp. 896–937.

Sontag, Susan (2009 [1966]), *Against Interpretation*, London: Penguin.

Tarr, Carrie (2012), 'Introduction: Women's Film-making in France 2000–2010', in *Studies in French Cinema* 12: 3 (October), 189–200.

Tarr, Carrie with Rollet, Brigitte (2001), *Cinema and the Second Sex*, London: Continuum Books.

Taylor, Charles (2007), *A Secular Age*, Cambridge, MA and London: Harvard University Press.

Turner, Edith (2012), *Communitas: The Anthropology of Collective Joy*, New York: Palgrave Macmillan.

Watkins, Robert E. (2008), 'Vulnerability, Vengeance, and Community: Butler's Political Thought and Eastwood's *Mystic River*', in Terrell Carver and Samuel A. Chambers (eds), *Judith Butler's Precarious Politics: Critical Encounters*, London and New York: Routledge, pp. 188–203.

Wheatley, Catherine (2016), 'An Autumn Tale', *Sight and Sound* 26: 9 (September), 24–7.

Wheatley, Catherine (2019), '"My Heart Inclines Wholly to Know Where is the True Good": Mia Hansen-Løve's post secular search for God', *Paragraph* 41: 3 (November), 316–32.

Wilson, Emma (2003), *Cinema's Missing Children*, London: Wallflower Press.

Wilson, Emma (2005), 'Children, Emotion and Viewing in Contemporary European Film', *Screen* 46: 3, 329–40.

Wilson, Emma (2006), 'Women Filming Children', *Nottingham French Studies* 45: 3, 105–18.

Wilson, Emma (2007), 'Miniature Lives, Intrusion and Innocence: Women Filming Children (2)', *French Cultural Studies* 18: 2, 169–83.

Wilson, Emma (2012), 'Precarious lives: On girls in Mia Hansen-Løve and others', *Studies in French Cinema* 12: 3, 273–84

Zeppenfeld, Axel (2007), 'Entretien avec Mia Hansen-Løve', *Cahiers du cinéma* 627 (October), p. 21.

French press reviews of Hansen-Løve's films

Azoury, Philippe (2014), 'L'Eden, et après', *Le Nouvel Observateur*, 25 September.

Blottière, Mathilde (2011), 'Mia Hansen-Løve dans l'ombre des jeunes filles en fleurs', *Télérama*, 6 July.

Blondeau, Romain (2014), 'French (re)Touch', *Les Inrockuptibles*, 8 January.

D.F. (2014), review of *Eden*, *Le Canard enchainé*, 19 November.

E.H. (2007), 'Vies de familles', *Les Echos*, 1 October.

Gandillot, Thierry (2014), 'Les souffrances du jeune raveur', *Les Echos*, 19 November.

Gester, Julien & Didier Péron (2014), 'Anomalie' (on *Eden*), *Libération*, 19 November.

Lepastier, Joachim (2014), 'Loin du paradis', *Cahiers du cinéma* 705, p. 28.

Lalanne, Jean-Marc (2007), review of *All Is Forgiven*, *Les Inrockuptibles*, 26 September.

Lalanne, Jean-Marc (2009), '*Le Père de mes enfants*, un portrait sensible et touchant', *Les Inrockuptibles*, 16 December.

Lalanne, Jean-Marc (2014a), 'Etoiles du Nord' (on *Eden*), *Les Inrockuptibles*, 24 September.

Lalanne, Jean-Marc (2014b), review of *Eden*, *Les Inrockuptibles*, 19 November.

Libiot, Eric (2014), 'Electro . . . un peu', *L'Express*, 19 November.

Maillard, Florence (2011), 'Le temps des sentiments', *Cahiers du cinéma* 668 (June), 50–2.

Mandelbaum, Jacques (2011), 'L'amour, expérience universelle et secrète', *Le Monde*, 6 July.

Morice, Jacques (2011), review of *Goodbye First Love* in *Télérama*, 6 July.

Renou-Nativel, Corinne (2018) '*Maya*, les fuites d'un grand reporter', *La Croix*, 19 December.

Widermann, Dominique (2014), 'Mia Hansen-Løve fait sonner la fin du party', *L'Humanité*, 19 November.

Film reviews by Hansen-Løve in *Cahiers du cinéma*

'Portraits crachés' (review of *Ken Park*), *Cahiers du cinéma* 583 (October 2003), 23–4.

'Jonas Mekas et le son retrouvé', *Cahiers du cinéma* 586 (January 2004), 71.

'Nous avons besoin d'action', Interview with Jonas Mekas, *Cahiers du cinéma* 587 (February 2004), 74–7.

'Exploration aux frontières', *Cahiers du cinéma* 589 (April 2004), 48–9.

'Zone Chine', *Cahiers du cinéma* 589 (April 2004), 23–6.

'Shanghai s'entrouvre aux cinéastes indépendants', *Cahiers du cinéma* 592 (July-August 2004), 64.

'Le Mékong vu du Tessin', *Cahiers du cinéma* 593 (September 2004), 52.

'Des jumelles et des jumeaux', *Cahiers du cinéma* 596 (December 2004), 51–2.

'Femmes de Mann', *Cahiers du cinéma* 597 (January 2005), 80–1.

'Cabengo', *Cahiers du cinéma* 598 (February 2005), 76–7.

'Echec et smash', *Cahiers du cinéma* 605 (July 2005), 28–9.

'Offensive sur les bords', *Cahiers du cinéma* 606 (August 2005), 29–30.

'Les passants et les passeurs', *Cahiers du cinéma* 604 (September 2005), 89–90.

'J'ai retrouvé l'homme dont je viens', *Cahiers du cinéma* 607 (December 2005), 34.

Presentation of *Tout est pardonné/All Is Forgiven*, *Cahiers du cinéma* 623 (May 2007), 22.

Radio

Hors Champs, broadcast on France Culture, 20 May 2010. An interview with Hansen-Løve by Laure Adler included on the DVD of *Goodbye First Love*.

Internet

'La place des femmes dans l'industrie cinématographique et audio-visuelle', on the CNC website at <https://www.cnc.fr/cinema/ etudes-et-rapports/etudes-prospectives/la-place-des-femmes-dans-lindustrie-cinematographique-et-audiovisuelle_300828> (last accessed 1 December 2018).

Filmography

Hansen-Løve as director

Après mûre refléxion/After Much Thought, film. Paris: Récifilms, 2004.
Isabelle par elle-meme/Isabelle By Herself, film, 2004.
Tout est pardonné/All Is Forgiven, film. Paris: Les Films Pelléas, 2007.
Le père de mes enfants/Father of My Children, film. Paris: Les Films Pelléas, 2009.
Un amour de jeunesse/Goodbye First Love, film. Paris : Les Films Pelléas & Berlin: Razor Film Produktion GmbH, 2011.
Eden, film. Paris: CG Cinéma, 2014.
L'Avenir/Things to Come, film. Paris: CG Cinéma, 2016.
Maya, film. Paris: Les Films Pelléas, 2018.
Bergman Island, film. Paris: Arte France Cinéma & CG Cinéma, forthcoming, 2021.

Other films

Ali, film, dir. Michael Mann. Culver City, CA: Columbia Pictures, 2001.
Collateral, film, dir. Michael Mann. Los Angeles, CA: Paramount Pictures & Universal City, CA: DreamWorks, 2004.
Elephant, film, dir. Gus van Sant. Santa Monica, CA: HBO Films, 2003.
Fin août, début septembre/Late August, Early September, film, dir. Oliver Assayas. Paris: Dacia Films, 1998.
Heat, film, dir. Michael Mann. Burbank, CA: Warner Bros, 1994.
It Follows, film, dir. David Robert Mitchell. Northern Lights Films, 2014.
Journal d'un curé de campagne/Diary of a Country Priest, film, dir. Robert Bresson. Neuilly-sur-Seine, Union Générale Cinématographique, 1951.
Ken Park, film, dir. Larry Clark. Cinéa, Kasander Film Company, Lou Yi Inc. & Marathon, 2002.

La fille prodigue/The Prodigal Daughter, film, dir. Jacques Doillon. Paris: Les Productions de la Guéville, 1981.

Lancelot du lac/Lancelot of the Lake, film, dir. Robert Bresson. Laser Productions, 1974.

Le diable probablement/The Devil Probably, film, dir. Robert Bresson. G.M.F Productions as G.M.F./M Chamberli & Sunchild Productions, 1977.

Les déstinées sentimentales/Les déstinées, film, dir. Olivier Assayas. Arcade, 2000.

Les quatre cents coups/The 400 Blows, film, dir. François Truffaut. Paris: Les Films du Carrosse, 1959.

Ma nuit chez Maud/My Night at Maud's, film, dir. Eric Rohmer. FFD & Les Films de la Pléiade, 1969.

Match Point, film, dir. Woody Allen. London: BBC Films, 2005.

Mystic River, film, dir. Clint Eastwood. Burbank, CA: Warner Bros, 2003.

Naissance des pieuvres/Waterlilies, film, dir. Céline Sciamma. Paris: Balthazar Productions, 2007.

Palais Royal!, film, dir. Valérie Lemercier. Paris: Gaumont & Rectangle Productions, 2005.

Partie de campagne/A Day in the Country, film, dir. Jean Renoir. Panthéon Productions, 1946.

Pickpocket, film, dir. Robert Bresson. Compagnie Cinématographique de France, 1959.

Poto and Cabengo, film, dir. Jean-Pierre Gorin. Jean-Pierre Gorin Productions & ZDF (Zweites Deutsches Fernsehen), Mainz, Germany, 1980.

Showgirls, film, dir. Paul Verhoeven. Carolco Pictures, 1995.

Un condamné à mort s'est echappé/A Man Escaped, film, dir. Robert Bresson. Paris: Gaumont & Nouvelles Editions de Films (NEF), 1956.

Un enfant dans la foule/A Child in the Crowd, film, dir. Gérard Blain. Cinépol & Renn Productions, 1976.

Index